Whitewater Home Companion

Southeastern Rivers

Volume I

Whitewater Home Companion

Southeastern Rivers

Volume I

By William Nealy

Menasha Ridge Press Birmingham, Alabama

Library of Congress Cataloging-in-Publication Data
Nealy, William, 1953-
      Whitewater home companion, southeastern rivers.
          1. White-water canoeing–Southern States–Guide-books.
2. Southern States–Description and travel–1951- –
Guide-books. I. Title.
GV776.S65N43   917.5   81-9854
ISBN 0-89732-028-X   AACR2

Menasha Ridge Press
3169 Cahaba Heights Road
Birmingham, AL 35243

This book is dedicated to
Louise Nealy
who knew I could

Acknowledgments

Special thanks to everyone in the paddling community who gave me so much time, assistance, and information in the course of making the maps and book. Thanks to Bob Sehlinger, who asked me to do the book, and to my editor, Holland Wallace, who made me do it. And finally, thanks to my paddling partner, Henry Unger, who hasn't gotten too mad about all the cancelled paddling trips and racquetball games....

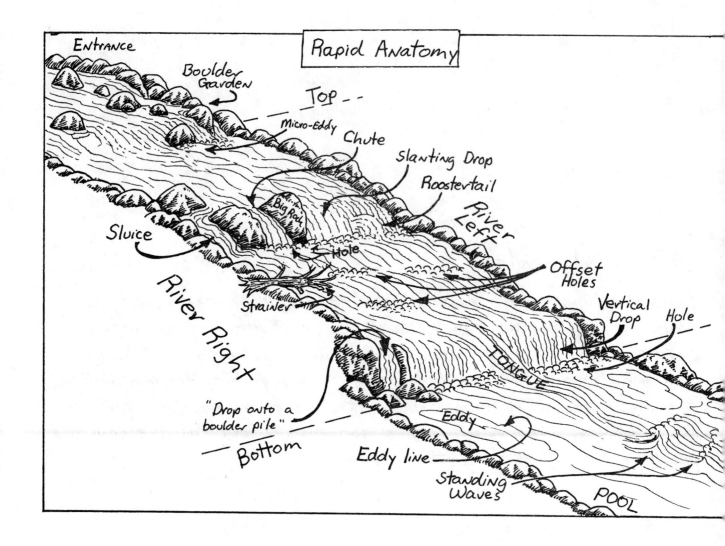

Rapid Anatomy

Entrance

Boulder Garden

TOP

Micro-Eddy   Chute

Slanting Drop

Roostertail

River Left

Big Rock

Sluice

Hole

Offset Holes

Vertical Drop

Hole

Strainer

River Right

TONGUE

"Drop onto a boulder pile"

Bottom

Eddy

Eddy line

Standing Waves

POOL

Contents

Introduction

Kayaks to Hell....

Whitewater boating has been around for quite some time. Independently invented by aboriginal cultures all over the world, before the invention of the wheel and the cocktail party, negotiating rapids was a necessary evil that had to be overcome in order to use rivers as roads. As good roads came along, primitive mankind gleefully ditched their river crafts and bought cars. Before World War II, whitewater boating as a sport was kind of a crank activity, akin to butterfly collecting and amateur Egyptology. During the 50's, some river runners began discovering that people would actually pay money to get wet and scared to death. A new industry was born. Along came the baby boom babies, looking for fun and excitement and, all of a sudden, masochism became really BIG BUSINESS.

"What?!" you say, "Boating is _fun_. What's all this neo-Freudian crapola about masochism anyway? Sounds like a bad attitude to me!" Maybe you're right, BUT when you get into year-round compulsive river-running, "fun" must be redefined. The idyllic summertime runs with warm water and beautiful women lounging on the rocks (hopefully "oohing" & "ahing" your surfing technique, perhaps offering you a sip of wine or a cool beer in some secluded eddy) are few and far between. Mostly it's sitting in a steamy smelly car with four other codevolutionists dressed in silly rubber suits, waiting for the snow to quit so you can do the first winter descent of some godforsaken little mountain stream. Or it's cringing as you hear your paddling buddy tell the "death run on the Suchnsuchee River" story for the fifth time this trip. I could go on. Being a whitewater addict is no bed of roses.

Boating is also a good excuse to dress up in ridiculous costumes and engage in bizzare rituals. An anthropologist from Borneo would have a field day analyzing whitewater boating as a quasi-religious death cult. Admittedly we do have an esoteric language, holy documents, high priests and priestesses, a rigid caste system, ritualized behavior and occasional human sacrifice. Mecca is Wesser, N.C. My mother once told me that even though she worried about me on these rivers, whitewater boating was better than being a Moonie. Little does she know.

Most of what I'm going to say in the rest of this book is my opinion of things white and watery. Some of the techniques described herein are things I've picked up in the last seven years that sometimes work for me. Most of the stories are true (the names have been changed to protect the guilty). I am not advocating that the American Whitewater Association adopt my suggestions, ideas, and terminology — it would be a tragic mistake! If you read this as a kind of a psychoanalytic case history of a deranged adrenaline addict, you will not go wrong.

Bon Appetit.

SPAWNING KAYAKS

River Trip

And it never ends........

4

Glossary, Terminology, Slang

Glossary — Continued

Glossary, slang terms, and terminology

backender — a backwards ender, with the stern of the boat getting pulled under instead of the bow. These can occur accidentally when you hit a wave or hole too slow to punch through. The best way to get backenders intentionally is to backpaddle on steep waves, lean back and hold on! [SEE ENDER]

bad — good, although sometimes "bad" is bad.

boat scouting — inspecting a rapid from your boat by eddy-hopping and running it in stages. On very steep drops, boat scouting is pretty useless in detecting strainers, bad holes, etc. Boat scouting should be done with discretion, scouting really steep stuff from the shore [See - SCOUTING].

boulder — an extra big rock (VW sized and up).

boulder garden — a rapid or shoal ornamented with lots of boulders.

canoe — A.K.A. "open boat" — Everyone knows what a canoe is; they may not know that canoes can run virtually anything a raft or decked boat can, in the hands of an expert canoeist. A variety of hull designs and materials are available. A.B.S. is the best choice of hull materials for all purpose river running [See CANOEIST]

canoeist — see "open boater."

C-boat — see "C-boater", "decked canoes."

C-boater — Anyone who paddles a C-1 or C-2 [see "decked canoes"] Easily recognized on the river — they're the ones crawling around on their hands

9

and knees at the lunch-stop beach because their legs fell asleep an hour ago. Even more obnoxious than their open boat cousins, expert c-boaters generally think kayakers are wimps, period.

cfs - cubic feet per second. Refers to the volume of water passing an established point of reference. Determined by taking depth readings across the river and calculating a two dimensional plane of reference. By applying water velocity readings to this plane, cfs is calculated. For example, a reading of 10,000 cfs means every second, 10,000 cubic feet of water pass the gauging point.

creek - a.k.a. "RUN" - a diminutive river.

crunchola - what happens when you miss the chute and end up on the rocks.

decked canoe - A single person decked canoe is referred to as a "C-1"; a two person decked canoe is a "C-2". Most non-boaters think C-1 paddlers are kayakers with half a paddle. The differences between a C-1 & a kayak are: ① C-1 spelled backwards is "1-C", ② you kneel in a C-1, you sit in a kayak. ③ C-1 & C-2 paddlers use a single-bladed paddle, kayakers use double-bladed paddles. ④ The C-1 roll is a two-step affair, ending on a low brace, a kayak roll is one step & ends on a high brace.

I said watch out for that rock, bozo!

WOOSH

C-1

C-2

drop - any vertical change in the riverbed that is perpendicular. Drops greater than 6' high are usually referred to as "falls" or "waterfall".

Glossary - Continued

drugs — Besides seriously impairing your ability to run whitewater, they're almost impossible to keep dry on the river.

dynamic — as in "dynamic eddy", "dynamic peel-out", "dynamic pool" etc. An extreme form of anything; a "dynamic eddy" would be a whirlpool or a bad hole. Used as a prefix, "dynamic" can turn the most mundane whitewater term into a highly colorful expression. Use your imagination.... dynamic lunch stop !?!

Dynamic Ender

eat it — to fall over or take a nasty swim. Variations include: "body-surfed", "chewed", "creamed" "crunched", "douched", "eaten", "mangled", "mashed", "munched", "mutilated", "pureed", "spewed", "stuffed", "thrashed", "trashed", "whipped", "woofed", etc.

eddy — relatively quiet spots found on the downstream side of rocks, pilings, rock formations, etc. In rapids, eddies are the boater's sanctuary. On flood-stage rivers, eddies can become whirlpools or bizzare boat naps —[see EDDY FENCE, FUNNY WATER]

eddy fence — the interface between the downstream flow and the eddy current; an eddy fence is a high-water phenomenon wherein the eddy becomes superelevated in relation to the main flow. The eddy line becomes a violent seething mess. Particularly rough on swimmers, the interface can pull you under and recirculate you like a hole.

eddy line — the normal-water line of transition between the main current and the slower, calmer eddy. Crossing an eddy line can be very exciting if you forget to anticipate the abrupt change in direction of flow the instant you cross the line.

11

ender- A.ka. "pop up", Western variation "endo". Many boaters make a distinction between enders & pop ups. I always get confused as to which is which, so I refer to both as "enders". An ender is caused by the bow of the boat getting pushed deep under the water, causing the boat to stand on end. The buoyancy of the boat then pushes it up and out. A good ender is when you get shot completely out of the water. A great ender is when you land on a raft! Decked boats are the preferred ender craft, although open boats are occasionally capable of it, (usually accidentally). You can get enders in holes, waves, and chutes. For hole enders, simply paddle upstream into the steepest part of the hole. If the hole is deep enough, you'll either ender out or get sucked into it for an extended surf. If its too shallow, you blow the nose off your boat. For waves, find a steep standing or breaking wave, surf out to the peak of it and drive the bow upstream into the trough. If you lean foreward, you'll probably do a long-axis flip. By leaning back and keeping your body perpendicular to the water, you may land upright. A good roll & lots of practice help. [SEE BACKENDER]

Glossary - Continued

entrapment - [see PINNED] - This is getting stuck in or out of your boat in fast-moving water. A very serious life-threatening situation requiring an immediate well-executed rescue. A boat entrapment happens when the boat pins and the deck (or hull) collapses, trapping the paddler in his or her boat. Even if the boat doesn't actually fold, the force of the water striking the paddler can prevent the paddler from getting out of the boat. In either case, immediate rescue is necessary to prevent drowning and/or hypothermia. Foot entrapments occur when the victim gets his/her foot caught in a crack or between two rocks. The force of the current holds the body under and drowning occurs quickly. The best way to avoid foot entrapment is by keeping your feet on the surface of the water pointed downstream when swimming a rapid. Never attempt to wade in or across a fast current. Never drag your feet across the bottom when trying to stand up in moving water. The best information available on entrapment and entrapment rescue techniques is published in the _River Safety Task Force News-Letter_, edited by Charlie Walbridge. Available from Wildwater Designs, Ltd., 230 Penllyn Pike, Penllyn, Pa. 19422

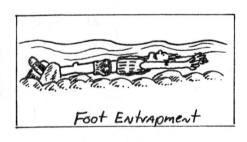

Foot Entrapment

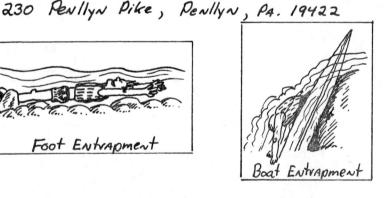

Boat Entrapment

Legal entrapment

EEK!

Eskimo Roll - A self-rescue technique practiced regularly by competant paddlers of decked boats. The eskimo roll is not that difficult to learn and once you perfect it, it will save you lots of wear & tear on your boat and body. It is best to learn in a pool or lake and graduate to moving water once you are semi-proficient at it. Once proficient on the river, practice fast rolling in "safe" rapids so that when you flip just above a monster hole you can roll up before you go into it.

Kayak Roll   C-boat roll

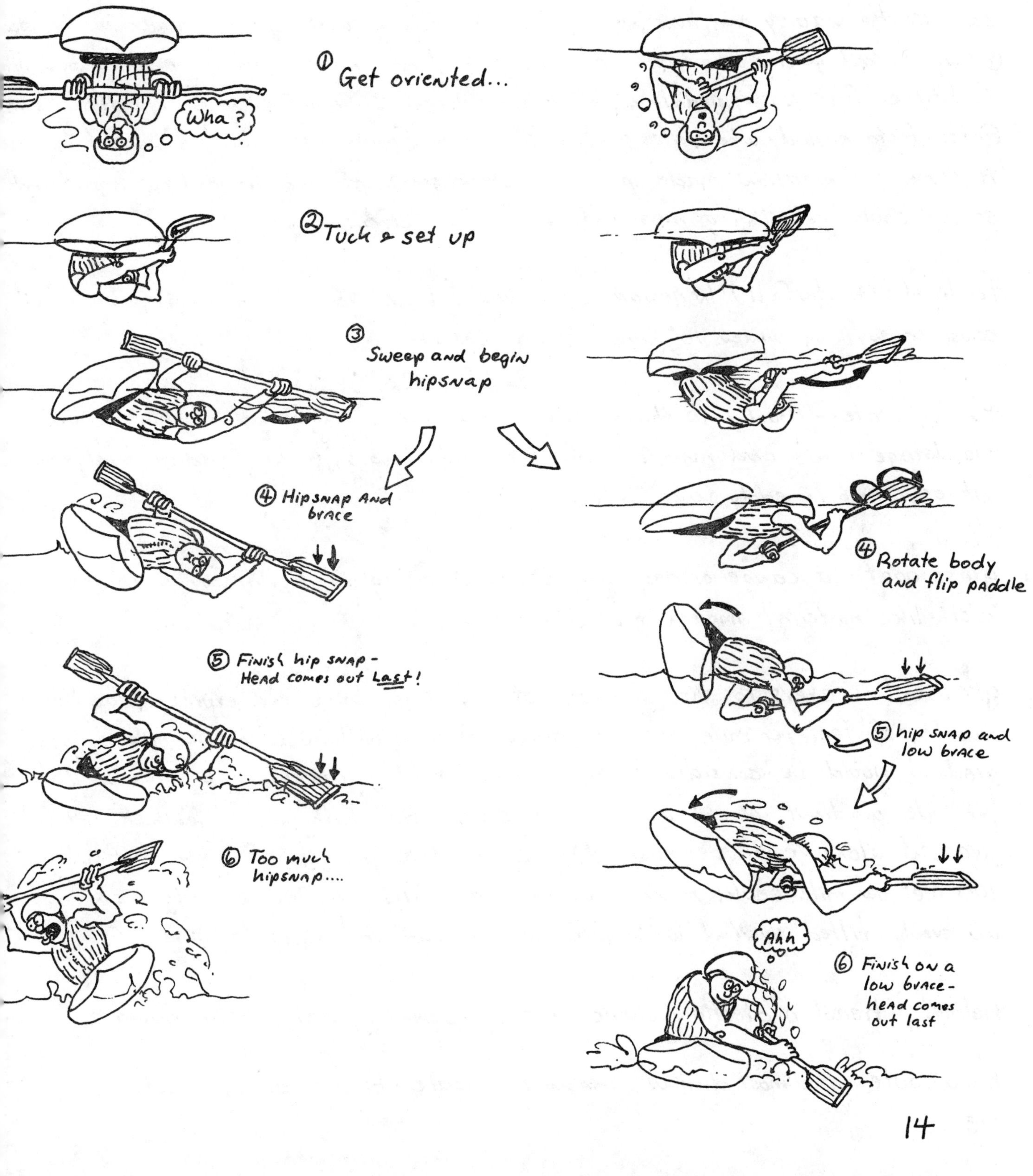

① Get oriented...

② Tuck & set up

③ Sweep and begin
    hipsnap

④ Hipsnap and
    brace

④ Rotate body
    and flip paddle

⑤ Finish hip snap -
    Head comes out Last!

⑤ hip snap and
    low brace

⑥ Too much
    hipsnap....

Ahh

⑥ Finish on a
    low brace-
    head comes
    out last

Wha?

14

Glossary - Continued

expert boater - usually a self-conferred title, qualifications for "expert boater" are nebulous and vary considerably. An "expert" can be: ① Any boater who paddles the Gauley and lives, ② Anyone who owns or works at a whitewater specialty store ③ Any decked boater who rolls up 50% of the time and does not get maimed or killed in his/her first year of paddling, ④ Any river guide, ⑤ Any raft guide, ⑥ Any outfitter, and ⑦ Ipso facto, anybody who writes guidebooks or makes maps, etc., etc.,. It would be nice if some organization made up some "expert" standards and handed out expert cards so we could establish a meaningful pecking order....

falls - (or waterfall). In general, any vertical drop over 6' in height. Purists don't consider anything under 10' high to be a waterfall.

funny water - Usually anything but. Funny water is found on high volume or floodstage rivers and manifests itself as whirlpools, boiling eddies, exploding waves, mobile eddy fences, etc.

glass boat - a canoe or decked boat made of fiberglass, kevlar, or any other cloth-like material impregnated with a resin.

gradient - refers to the steepness of the river bed and expressed as the number of feet per mile the river drops. A river with a 15 foot per mile average gradient would be considered to have a "mild" gradient. One with a 75' per mile gradient would be a fairly steep river. Although somewhat helpful, gradient alone can be misleading as a true gauge of river difficulty. 100 feet per mile could mean two 50' waterfalls or 200 6" ledges, or an evenly tilted riverbed with swift water and no rapids to speak of.

helmet - head protection device - a.k.a. beanie, hat, brain bucket.

hero route - the most difficult imaginable route thru a given rapid.

hole - see hydraulic

hot dog - expert paddler or a beginner with a death wish.

hydraulic - A.ka. "hole", "sousehole", "vertical eddy", "reversal", "soup". Caused
by water flowing over an obstacle (such as a rock, ledge, dam, etc.)
and creating a reversal current. Hydraulics
come in a variety of shapes and sizes but the
mechanism is always the same: the velocity of
the water passing over the obstruction is far
greater than the water velocity below the hole, creating a region of surplus water
with nowhere to go. Via friction this surplus water is pulled/pushed back upstream
becoming aeriated where the flows interface (A diagram). When our hypothetical swimmer
hits point A, he is sucked under and begins to get recirculated along A→B→C→A. Unless
he dives deep into the water still flowing downstream D, he will remain in the hole. A
rescuer would have a good chance to pluck him out when he resurfaces at C
and begins moving upstream again. If the rescuer crosses the peak of the boil at C
he too will end up in the hole. [See Hole Escape Techniques].

    In general, the severity of any hole is directly proportional to the width of
the hole, the steepness of the drop, and the depth of the hole (Nastiness Theorum).
The steeper the drop, the wider the hole, or the deeper the hole, the worse
the hydraulic. Low dams and some wide ledges combine all three principles for
maximum nastiness. Since swimming to the side of a hole (in the hope that
you'll get pulled out by the downstream current at the hole's edge) is one of the
only means of self rescue you have, dams are particularly bad because there
is no surface downstream current to swim to. If you get caught in a wide symmetrical
hydraulic such as a dam reversal, just about your only hope is to swim out
by diving into the deep downstream current (D) and resurfacing below pt. C. This is
perhaps the only case where shedding your p.f.d. might help BUT only as a last

16

Glossary - Continued

resort. That deep downstream current is very powerful and, likely as not, will bounce you across the rocks on the bottom, possibly knocking you out. Shedding your P.F.O. is an act of extreme desperation and cannot be recommended!

   Some holes can be surfed safely, others shouldn't even be run. The good surfing holes are generally the big violent-looking things that are not much wider than the length of a boat. The violence of the hole can be an indication of a good downstream flow, not too deep below the reversal.* You may get recirculated once but chances are the power of the deep flow will carry you far below the boil before you resurface. Keep in mind, these are observations, not rules! There are many many exceptions to what is being described here. In general, it's the comparatively calm-looking highly-aeriated holes that are the worst keepers. Any particularly bad hole is referred to as a "terminal hole" or "keeper."

Symmetrical Hole (low dam)
Note crest of the boil is far downstream

Convex Hole
Escape at either edge

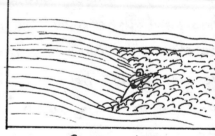

Concave Hole
- Very difficult to get out of

Holes also make great dynamic eddies... good for a few seconds of relatively calm water if you land in the backwash. If you stay in too long and get sucked into the hole itself, the hole may be referred to as a "keeper eddy."

   * On the opposite page is a photo of a kayak in "Hell Hole" on the Ocoee River. This is a particularly violent-looking hole that may stop you and toss you out to the left. It is not a keeper. 50 yards below Hell Hole is the wide keeper hole in Powerhouse Rapid. [See Ocoee River map]

Hell Hole at 1,350 c.fs., Ocoee R.

William Nealy Photo

Kayak - A.K.a. "yak", "K-1" - Without a doubt the most versatile, dynamic, and enjoyable river craft of all. Despite what open boaters & C-1 paddlers think of them, Kayaks are highly maneuverable, fast, tricky, and take a high degree of skill to master. [see ESKIMO ROLL] Kayakers sit inside the boat and use a two-bladed

Kayak

Glossary - Continued

paddle. Kayaks are available in a huge variety of hull designs, from low-volume radically-designed slalom racers to high-volume plastic monsters. Kayaks are usually made of fiberglass, plastic ("tupperware"), or A.B.S.. Substantial internal bracing is necessary to prevent deck collapse. Additional floatation (air-bags) should always be used. Until you master the eskimo roll, river running should be limited to "safe", easy rivers. My favorite book for kayak technique is <u>Kayaking,</u> <u>the New Whitewater Sport for Everybody</u> by Jay Evans and Bob Anderson (Stephen Greene Press) — an excellent teaching/learning manual!

Kayakers— Anyone who paddles a kayak. Easily recognizable by their graceful finesse, and seemingly divine inspiration, expert kayakers are far more tolerant and level-headed than their expert canoeist brothers and sisters (open & decked boats). The kayaker realizes the whole single-blade vs. double blade paddle controversy boils down to the canoeists' feelings of sexual inadequacy and insecurity. Expert kayakers never stoop to macho gamesmanship like their canoeist colleagues.

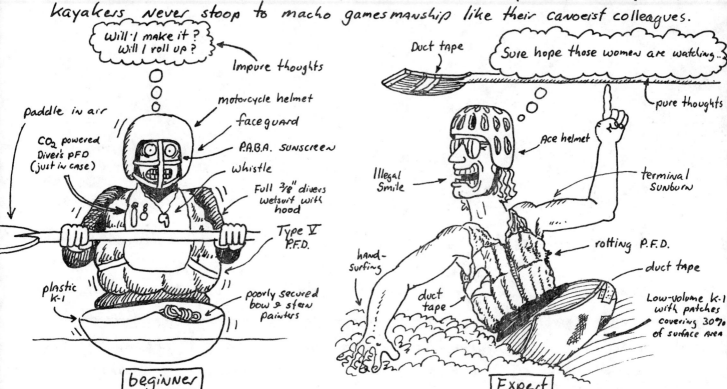

- A comparison of the typical beginner and the typical expert kayaker -

Keeper Eddy - hole used as an eddy [see HYDRAULIC]

local(s)-Aka "Natives" - Recognized by "Goin' fishin'?" or "What's that, a ski?" and similar questions. Or "Save A Job - Shoot An Environmentalist" bumperstickers. Locals are people indigenous to whatever area you happen to be in. The spectrum of locals' behavior is broad, ranging from overt hostility to down-home hospitality. Generally friendly when treated with dignity and respect. Locals in mountainous areas (particularly in the Bible Belt) tend to look upon whitewater boating as an activity somewhere between devil worship and heroin addiction.

lunch bunny - A.k.a. "female raft guide trainee" - Not to be confused with the true WOMAN raft guide, lunch bunnies are hired to provide a little tits & ass for the customers and to assure everybody that, even on the river, a woman's place is in the kitchen. Disgusting.

mega - means big or big-time. Interchangeable with "super" as a superlative prefix. Add to ANY word (ie: "mega-rock", "mega-hole") for mega-emphasis.

open boaters - A.k.a "canoeists" [see CANOE] - Anyone who paddles a canoe, single or tandem. Easily recognizeable for their habit of swimming Class IV rapids and thinking it's "fun". Frequently seen in the middle of the river trying frantically to peel their canoes off rocks. Usually heard yelling at their paddling partner about what he or she should have done. Expert open boaters can be recognized by their curious attitudes about Kayakers being untalented, irresponsible, subhuman rodents. Often heard saying, "Shit, that's EASY with two blades!". They are very sensitive about whether a canoe can run anything a kayak can. Of course, everybody knows they can, but these guys are still paranoid about it.

Glossary - Continued

peel out - pulling out of an eddy pointed upstream. When you cross the eddy line the downstream current snatches the bow of the boat and abruptly spins the boat around facing downstream. If you forget to apply a low brace on your downstream side plus a downstream lean, you will dynamically flip toward your upstream side.

pillow - a cushion of water on the upstream face of a rock or boulder. A "well-padded" boulder has a pillow that allows you to slide across the face of the rock without actually touching it. If the pillow is too thin, you get stuck on the upstream side of the rock. [see PIN]

pin - a form of entrapment; a pinned boat is a boat stuck or wedged in the river. A paddler stuck in a pinned boat is a pinned paddler. A pinning is a potentially fatal situation and rescue should be immediate. If you are in a pinned boat and cannot wiggle the boat free, it is generally best to bail out if you can, before the boat folds or submerges (that is, unless there's a 50' waterfall just below, in which case you're probably safer pinned).
[see ENTRAPMENT]

pirouette - an ender with a half-twist. When the boat stands on end, you twist around (possibly with the aid of a crossdraw) and land upright facing downstream.

pool - any relatively calm stretch of water just below a rapid. Any calm stretch of water not found just below a rapid is generally referred to as "a calm stretch of water".

put in - where ever you begin a river trip, ie: where you park the car and get in your boat.

raft - AKA. "rubber bus", "pig boat," etc. - An inflatable rubber boat used by commercial outfitters (mainly). No comment.

raft guide - man or woman in charge of the raft (commercial river trips). A.Ka. "guide", "boatman", Western variation - "captain". Raft guides either possess the serenity and infinite patience of a zen master or the demeanor of a riot cop. Some control the customers with a mixture of Monty Python and Captain Bligh, others would probably make good Marine drill instructors. Some of them crack up and become Jehovah's Witnesses or Insurance salesmen.

rafters - a.k.a. "customers", "pilgrims", [See TURKEY] Rafters are people who pay to get thrashed on rivers in unwieldy rubber boats while being screamed at by teenaged raft guides - and love it. Recognized by their insatiable desire to have constant water fights and yell at the top of their lungs. Frequently resented by private boaters, rafters do provide some of us with lots of cartoon ideas, occasional free lunches, and money.

river guide - male or female in decked or open boat that accompanys the raft trip and sets up safety ropes, gives directions, etc. The river guide is the envy of all the raft guides and is frequently seen engaged in daring and dangerous feats of skill (for the enjoyment of the customers).

Raft Guides' Tales of Terror, #3...

Ok guys, we're taking a church group down today, so NO cussing.

Which church?

Unification church, something like that.....

Oh shit

Glossary — Continued

river left — on the left, facing downstream. Since most all rivers flow only one way, this mode of direction eliminates lots of confusion. [see RIVER RIGHT]

river right — on the right, facing downstream.

rock garden — a rapid or shoal ornamented with lots of rocks.

roll — a small loaf of bread, usually baked. — Similar to a muffin or biscuit.

roostertail — caused by moving water striking a rock and spewing in an upwardly direction. The plume in the Ocoee's "Tablesaw" is a roostertail.

safety rope — Aka "rapid floss", "throw rope", "rescue rope" —
An essential piece of river running equipment, safety ropes should accompany any group down the river. Learning to properly use one takes instruction and practice. The throw-bag is a neat little item — it's basically a safety rope in a bag. You hold one end of the rope and throw the bag. If you have stuffed it in correctly, the rope will evenly feed out of the bag. Unlike a coil of

Improper use of Safety Rope
ROOOOPE!
PLOP!

rope, the throw bag is instantly available and requires no setting up prior to throwing it. Safety ropes are also very useful for boat recovery and impromptu boat-thief lynchings.

scouting — to visually inspect a rapid or drop. Any unfamiliar or very steep rapid should be scouted. Scouting is the best way to avoid river accidents and allows you to anticipate problems. Not scouting a rapid because you "know it" is not unlike playing with "unloaded" guns.

Shoal – a rather nebulous term referring to anything from a rock garden to a gravel bar. Usually a shallow, ledgy section with fast water and lots of rocks to get hung on.

Shuttle – What you do before and after the river trip. This involves putting a vehicle of some description at the takeout so you can get back to the vehicle you left at the put in. Bicycles, mopeds, and creative hitchhiking are alternatives to the traditional two-car shuttle. [SEE SHUTTLE BUNNY]

Shuttle bunny – Somebody's wife or girlfriend who runs shuttle for you while you have fun on the river. "Darlin', maybe I'd better paddle solo today... this river is tough!" Poof – instant shuttle bunny! They are true saints.

Sneak – to take the easiest (or safest) route through a rapid. Can also mean "to covertly portage a rapid". Aka. "chicken route", "tourist route", "girl scout route" – [SEE HERO ROUTE]

Speared – Aka. "harpooned" – Being speared is getting stabbed by either the bow or stern of a decked boat. Usually occurring in eddies and on surfing waves, getting speared is about as much fun as getting hit by a car. Radical low-volume racing boats (Lettman MK. VI, for example) are particularly hazardous, but any decked boat can do the job. Particularly pointy boats should have some form of padding on the bow to prevent injuries to other paddlers. Rafts are fair game.

Speared kayaker
Sorry Bud!
OOF!
THUK!

Stopper – either a hole or breaking wave that stops you dead and chews you up.

Glossary – Continued

strainer – Any obstacle in the river that allows water to pass through but not boats and people. Fallen trees, logs, river debris, chunks of metal, et al., are extremely dangerous if they lie in fast-moving water. Always give strainers a wide berth. If you ever do get washed into a strainer, lean downstream, into or onto the obstacle. This gives you the opportunity to climb onto it if you can't get clear.

surf – to ride a wave on its upstream face or to get stuck in a hole intentionally (or unintentionally). Surfing is a source of endless amusement for most boaters, open and decked. On real crowded rivers such as the Neu or the Ocoee, the overenthusiastic surfer will usually end up getting run over repeatedly by rafts. Hole surfing is easier than wave surfing because once you get in the hole, _it_ does all the work. The problem with hole-surfing is getting out without getting munched. [See "Hole Escape Techniques" To avoid shoulder dislocations from high bracing in holes, learn to surf holes on a low brace- it's less tiring, too.

take out – the place where you get out of the boats and into the cars.

tuber – a.k.a. "Hole bait", "Dead meat"- [see TURKEY]. A tuber is a root-like vegetable and/or someone who runs rivers in inner tubes (generally without the benefit of lifejackets, helmets, and common sense). The "sport" of inner-tubing is proof that natural selection is still at work. Given a few more generations, tubers will probably all but disappear. Tubers are usually seen throwing beer cans in the river and getting recirculated in nasty hydraulics.

turkey – [see rafter, tuber]- generic term for novice boaters, rafters, and tubers. To expert boaters, it describes everybody else.

tweeze- A.K.A. "thread the needle"- to take a tight route between two obstacles; also means to catch a tiny seam between big holes.

Walk the dog - to portage a rapid or to drag your boat.

Washed out- A high water phenomenon wherein the water is sufficiently deep to bury rocks and drops, simplifying entire rapids dramatically.

Wave- A wave is the result of gravity, mass, and water velocity. A wave is the direct expression of a river's energy. Waves come in a variety of shapes, sizes, and forms; they commonly range in size from 6" to 8'. Giant waves are a super high-volume phenomenon and, if you can believe the stories, get as high as 15 to 20 feet. Hmm.

Standing Waves- these are stationary waves in sets of two or more. Real big standing waves are called haystacks.

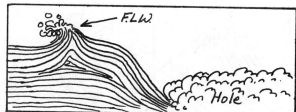

F.L.W. or "funny little wave"- small breaking or standing waves found just above certain types of holes

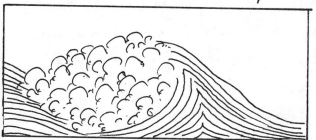

breaking wave- A.K.A "wave/hole"- Looks like a giant, violent hole and can stop a boat or raft. A breaking wave will almost never recirculate you.

curler- A wave that distinctly curves upstream at the top and breaks about a third of the way down the face.

Glossary - Continued

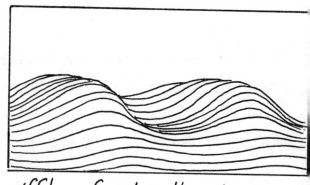

Lateral wave - a diagonal breaking wave. Lateral waves are usually caused by an obstruction just downstream. Always violent and tricky, lateral waves break on top of you and knock you sideways. Notorious raft flippers.

riffles - found in the entrance section of many rapids, where the river constricts and gains energy. Riffles are low and rounded, giving a rollercoasteresque ride.

KA-WUMP!

Exploding wave - a high water phenomenon, these monsters cycle and pulsate. The cycle starts with a standing wave (1) that gets higher & thicker until it curls over and breaks (2), then it collapses into a writhing violent hole-looking thing (3). The cycle begins as it builds back into a standing wave (1). Length of the cycle varies wave to wave. The object of the game is to time it so you go thru before or after the wave collapses. Exploding waves are frequently found below the normal terminus of a rapid (floodstage) where the current is suddenly decelerated and the river gives up its built-up energy.

tail waves - series of standing waves below rapids that begin large and taper out to nil. Usually good for surfing and playing.

27

Diagonal Wave - medium to high water phenomenon, diagonal waves are usually found at the tops of rapids and on sharp curves in the river. They look pretty harmless but a big one can easily flip a raft.

Reflex wave - similar to diagonal waves, a reflex wave is the river's response to obstructions in the main current. Most often found near steep river banks at high water, these waves can be diagonal or even parallel to the main current. Aka "bank waves".

Undercut Rock — any rock, boulder, or rock formation that has been eroded just beneath the surface of the water. Radical undercutting results in a mushroom-like formation, with the bottom of the cap just under water. Extremely dangerous for paddlers, undercut rocks are frequently jammed with logs and other river debris, creating particularly nasty

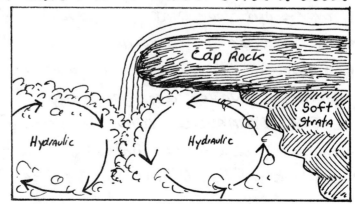

Undercut boulder   Undercut strainer

strainers. Sandstone is highly susceptible to radical undercutting, thus rivers such as the Gauley (which cut through sandstone beds) are chock full of undercut rocks. Undercut ledges are caused by erosion of the softer rock underlying the harder cap rock, creating a cave-like formation. Often a double hydraulic forms if the undercutting is drastic enough. The Chattooga's Sock-Em-Dog has a similar configuration. - bad medicine!

Cap Rock

Soft Strata

Hydraulic   Hydraulic

Hole Escape Techniques

At some point in everyone's river-running career, they end up stuck in a hole, one way or another. Some boaters, particularly of the decked boat variety, jump into holes every chance they get. As a member of the latter sub-set, I've attempted to surf some holes that just would not let go, period. These suggestions MAY work for you and they may not. In a particularly sticky hole you may get the chance to try each one of them before discovering an entirely new never-before-seen hole exiting technique.

Which holes can be surfed? Good question. I prefer the narrow-width violent type (hopefully not at the top of a Class IV rapid). It takes years of in-hole experience to be able to correctly guess the personality of each individual hole. Then there's always the hole that doesn't act the way you figured and you get munched real good. Consider it an ongoing learning experience. Perhaps the best way to decide whether or not to surf a given wave is to talk a friend into trying it first. That way you can see what would have happened to you had you not been so creatively empirical. Throwing driftwood or milk jugs into holes can tell you some things about a hole's nature but a milk jug just isn't you.

Breaking waves look and act just like holes. They are big & violent and will hold you as long as you stay upright and in your boat. Fall over & exit your boat and woosh!... you come up twenty yards downstream. Because the backwash is really a thin facade covering the upstream face of the wave, you land right in a good downstream current. Breaking waves are generally the best type of "hole" to surf in. [SEE HYDRAULIC, WAVE, -glossary]

In general; don't surf holes at the top of big rapids or just above 50' waterfalls. When you realize you're stuck, make your

Open boater executing an upstream dynamic roll hole-escape on a breaking wave.
Double Trouble, Ocoee River.

move early on, before you get exhausted. Surf on a low brace - it's much less tiring than high-bracing and it's virtually impossible to dislocate your shoulder on a low brace.

So, you're stuck in a hole sideways and you can't get out. First, switch to a low brace & smile at your friends so they'll think you really mean to be in there. Before your arms get too exhausted it's time to try to get out while remaining in your boat....

① Reverse sweep on the downstream side. Easily done from a low brace, reverse sweeping is plenty powerful and may push you out one side of the hole or the other. If you should get turned perpindicular to the backwash, drive foreward and try to ender out.

② Alternately foreward & reverse sweeping - this may rock you out at one end of the hole or the other.

③ Deep bracing - set up to roll on your downstream side, take a good breath and roll over on your downstream side. When you're upside-down, reach down ("up" to you) with your paddle & try to catch the downstream current down deep. The longer you stay upside-down the better your chances of getting pulled out. Rolling up isn't too difficult unless your paddle gets snatched out of your hands or you try to roll on the upstream side.

④ Popped-skirt dynamic submarine exit; I learned this by accident while trying to wet exit in a hole. Pop your skirt and let the boat fill up with water (hope you remembered your float bags!) When the boat is mostly full, brace yourself in and roll to the upstream side! [Note - if you're not really locked into your boat you'll be torn violently out of the cockpit at this point]. Your boat and you will probably disappear and travel quite some distance underwater before the stern pops up, followed by the rest of the boat and, hopefully, you. Not recommended for every-day use, this "method" does work 50% of the time.

⑤ Bumping — this is where another boat enters the hole to try to knock you out of it. Usually succeeds in providing the hole with some fresh meat. A.K.A. "Tag surfing". If both of you remain in the hole, things really get brutal — this is a very good time to think about swimming for it. Raft bumping usually occurs unintentionally. However, most paddlers prefer to remain stuck in the hole to being dragged around underneath a raft.

Bumping often creates more problems than it solves.

If all else fails, you can always try catching a safety rope, swimming for it, or becoming an innovative escape-technique artist!

Legend

Legend

The rating system —
Class I — Easy; small regular waves, clear passages, no maneuvering necessary.
Class II — slightly difficult; small drops, clear passages, no maneuvering necessary.
Class II-III — An easy rapid that requires maneuvering.
Class III — Difficult — numerous and irregular waves, narrow passages, significant drops. Requires maneuvering. Scouting advisable.
Class III-IV — A particularly difficult Class III or a "relatively easy" Class IV
Class IV — Very difficult — large irregular waves, crosscurrents, big drops, fast & powerful water. Requires precise maneuvering. Scouting manda...
Class IV-V — A particularly lengthy or difficult Class IV or an unusually straightforeward & "easy Class V-esque rapid.
Class V — Extremely difficult; Class IV^2! Huge irregular waves, fast and powerful current, violent holes & cross-currents, heavily obstructed riverbed, big drops. Precise maneuvering is a matter of surviva... Scouting mandatory!
Class VI — Ultimate limit of navigability — Class V^3! Danger of loss of life* — might possibly be run by a team of experts using all possible safety precautions.
Class VII (European Class VI) A Class VI that has never been run success... fully. For certifiably-insane experts.

---

*The "loss of life" clause has caused the Class VI rating to be used to signify a particularly dangerous rapid, not necessarily meaning the rapid is all that difficult technically. For example, Woodall Shoals on the Chattooga carries a Class VI rating because of its deadly hydraulic. Woodall Shoals is technically a Class III drop.

Rapid ratings given in parenthesis refer to increasing difficulty of some rapids at higher than normal water levels. Some rapids become washed out at high water and consequently get easier as the water rises. Some rapids get harder as the water level drops, resulting in a more technical rapid.

Overall river ratings give the average difficulty of the river taken as a whole. A river with 20 Class III's and one Class V would be designated as having an overall difficulty of Class III$_V$.

Routes through individual rapids are suggestions only! I rarely get the chance to run all possible routes through all rapids, so my route suggestions are not meant to preclude any other routes.

All directions given in rapid descriptions refer to "river right" or "river left" (see Glossary). Shuttle directions refer to "road left" or "road right", meaning on your right or left respectively as you approach the turn or landmark.

In all the maps I have used an elastic scale as a stylistic device to get my high-oblique perspective (Artistic License #0061). On most of the maps I've supplemented the scale elasticity with mile markers → (mile 2) or a mileage number in the description of each rapid.

On all the maps, the river flows from the top to the bottom of the page into your lap.

These maps are intended to enhance and supplement your river experience; not for use as a substitute for scouting, skill, good safety precautions, or good judgement.

34

Chattahoochee River

GEORGIA

CHATTAHOOCHEE

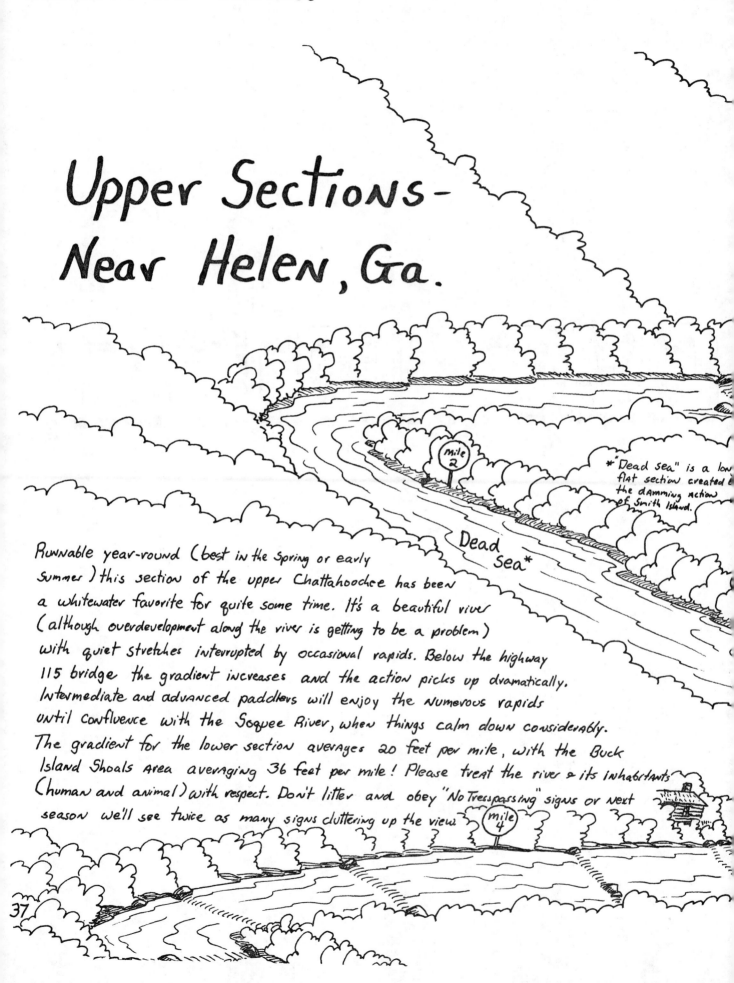

Upper Sections-
Near Helen, Ga.

*"Dead sea" is a long flat section created by the damming action of Smith Island.

Dead sea*

Runnable year-round (best in the spring or early summer) this section of the upper Chattahoochee has been a whitewater favorite for quite some time. It's a beautiful river (although overdevelopment along the river is getting to be a problem) with quiet stretches interrupted by occasional rapids. Below the highway 115 bridge the gradient increases and the action picks up dramatically. Intermediate and advanced paddlers will enjoy the numerous rapids until confluence with the Soquee River, when things calm down considerably. The gradient for the lower section averages 20 feet per mile, with the Buck Island Shoals area averaging 36 feet per mile! Please treat the river & its inhabitants (human and animal) with respect. Don't litter and obey "No Tresspassing" signs or next season we'll see twice as many signs cluttering up the view

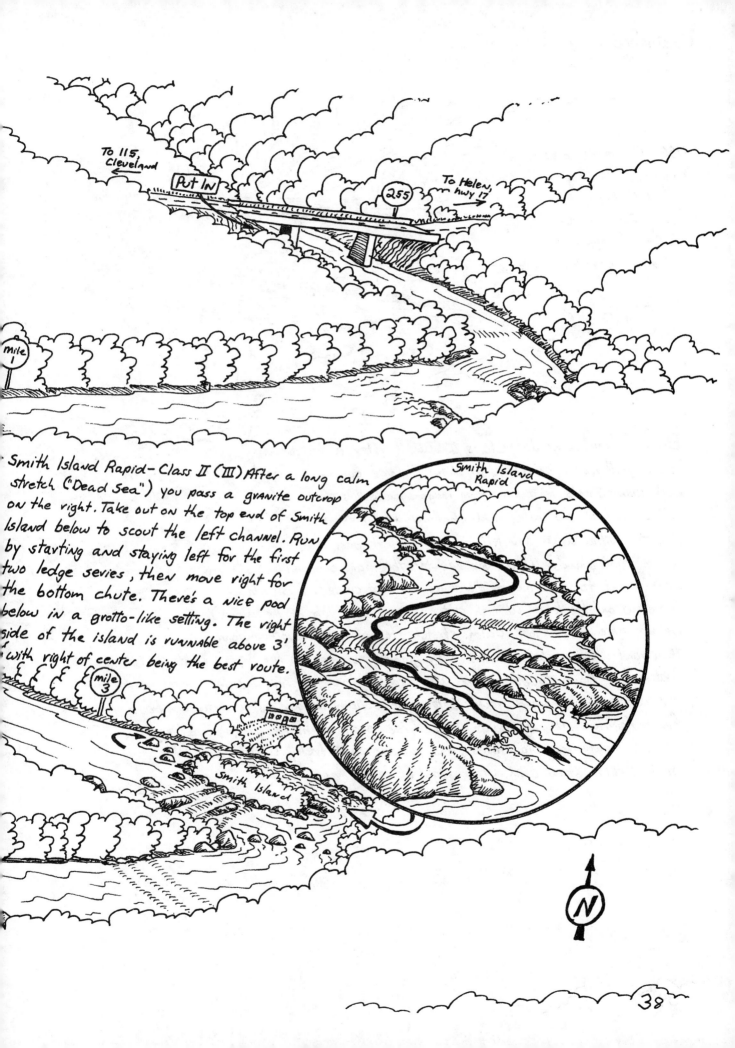

Smith Island Rapid – Class II (III) After a long calm
stretch ("Dead Sea") you pass a granite outcrop
on the right. Take out on the top end of Smith
Island below to scout the left channel. Run
by starting and staying left for the first
two ledge series, then move right for
the bottom chute. There's a nice pool
below in a grotto-like setting. The right
side of the island is runnable above 3'
with right of center being the best route.

To 115,
Cleveland

Put In

255

To Helen,
hwy 17

mile
1

Smith Island
Rapid

mile
3

Smith Island

N

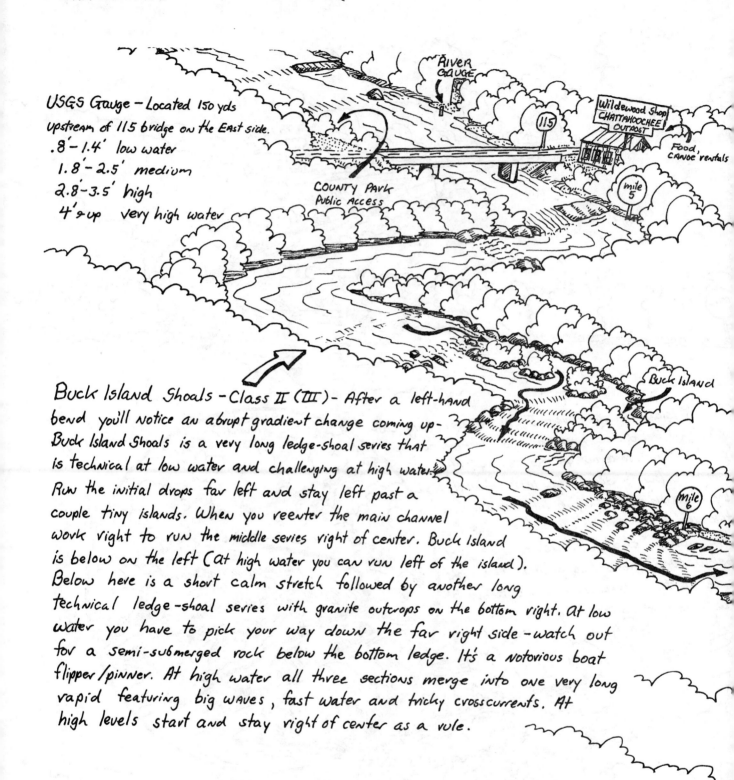

USGS Gauge — Located 150 yds
upstream of 115 bridge on the East side.
.8' – 1.4' low water
1.8' – 2.5' medium
2.8' – 3.5' high
4' & up   very high water

Buck Island Shoals — Class II (III) — After a left-hand
bend you'll notice an abrupt gradient change coming up—
Buck Island Shoals is a very long ledge-shoal series that
is technical at low water and challenging at high water.
Run the initial drops far left and stay left past a
couple tiny islands. When you reenter the main channel
work right to run the middle series right of center. Buck Island
is below on the left (at high water you can run left of the island).
Below here is a short calm stretch followed by another long
technical ledge-shoal series with granite outcrops on the bottom right. At low
water you have to pick your way down the far right side — watch out
for a semi-submerged rock below the bottom ledge. It's a notorious boat
flipper/pinner. At high water all three sections merge into one very long
rapid featuring big waves, fast water and tricky crosscurrents. At
high levels start and stay right of center as a rule.

Three Ledges – Class II-III (III) Beginning with a long class I shoal, granite outcrops (on the right) signal the first drop. Run this by going just left of a long low hot-dog shaped rock. Ferry right for the second ledge – a fun s-turn through some low broken ledges. Start right of center. After the second ledge, work back to the left. Third ledge is a riverwide vertical 3' drop extending from the island to the left shore. Run just left of the hump in the center for the best landing spot. If you go too far left you'll get to meet "Rainbow Rock", which bears the marks of hundreds of errant ABS canoes. The bottom-right side of the drop has a good surfing hole at most levels. The bottom-left of the hole is pretty grabby and tends to pull you in between Rainbow rock and the drop and hold you there.

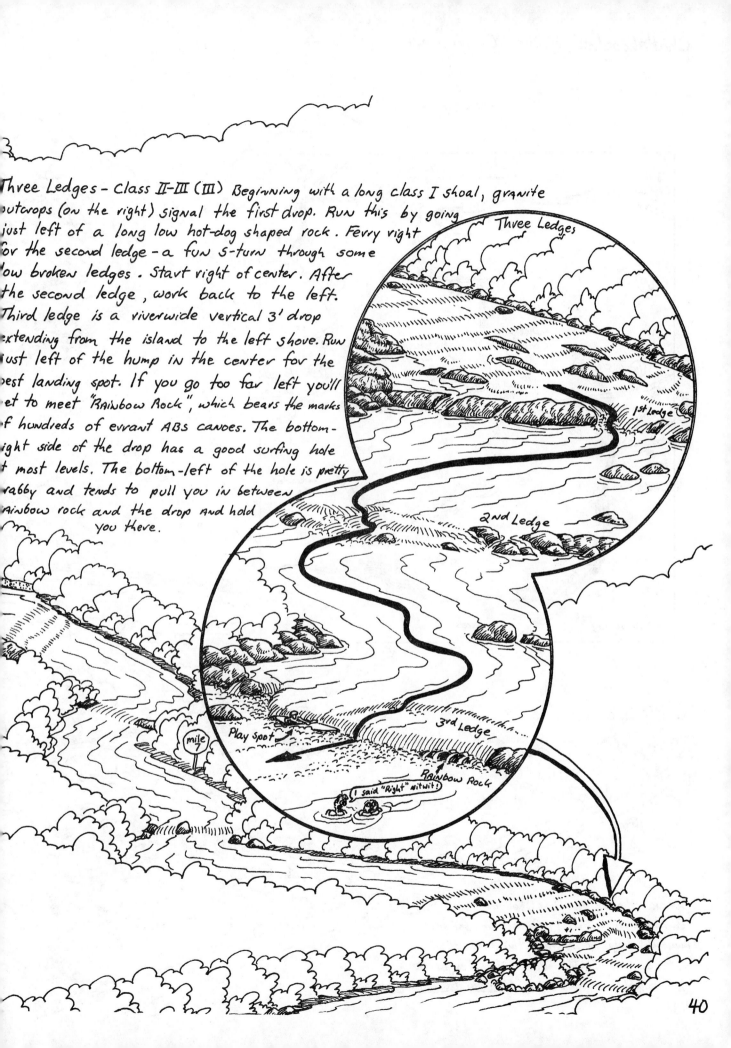

Three Ledges

1st Ledge

2nd Ledge

3rd Ledge

Rainbow Rock

Play spot

mile 7

I said "Right" nitwit!

40

Chattahoochee River - Continued

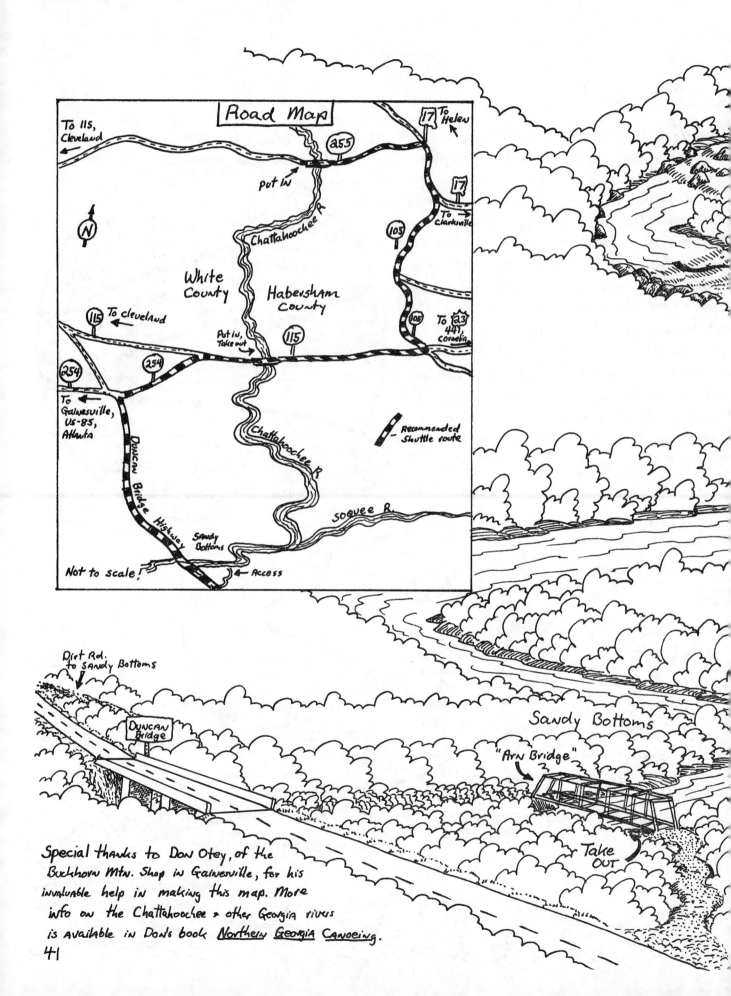

Road Map

To 115, Cleveland

17 To Helen

255

put in

17

To Clarksville

105

Chattahoochee R.

White County

Habersham County

115 To Cleveland

Put in, Take out

115

105

To 23, 441 Cornelia

254

254

To Gainesville, US-85, Atlanta

Duncan Bridge Highway

Chattahoochee R.

Recommended Shuttle route

Soquee R.

Sandy Bottoms

Not to scale!

Access

N

Dirt Rd. to Sandy Bottoms

Duncan Bridge

Sandy Bottoms

"Arn Bridge"

Take OUT

Special thanks to Don Otey, of the Buckhorn Mtn. Shop in Gainesville, for his invaluable help in making this map. More info on the Chattahoochee & other Georgia rivers is available in Don's book _Northern Georgia Canoeing_.

41

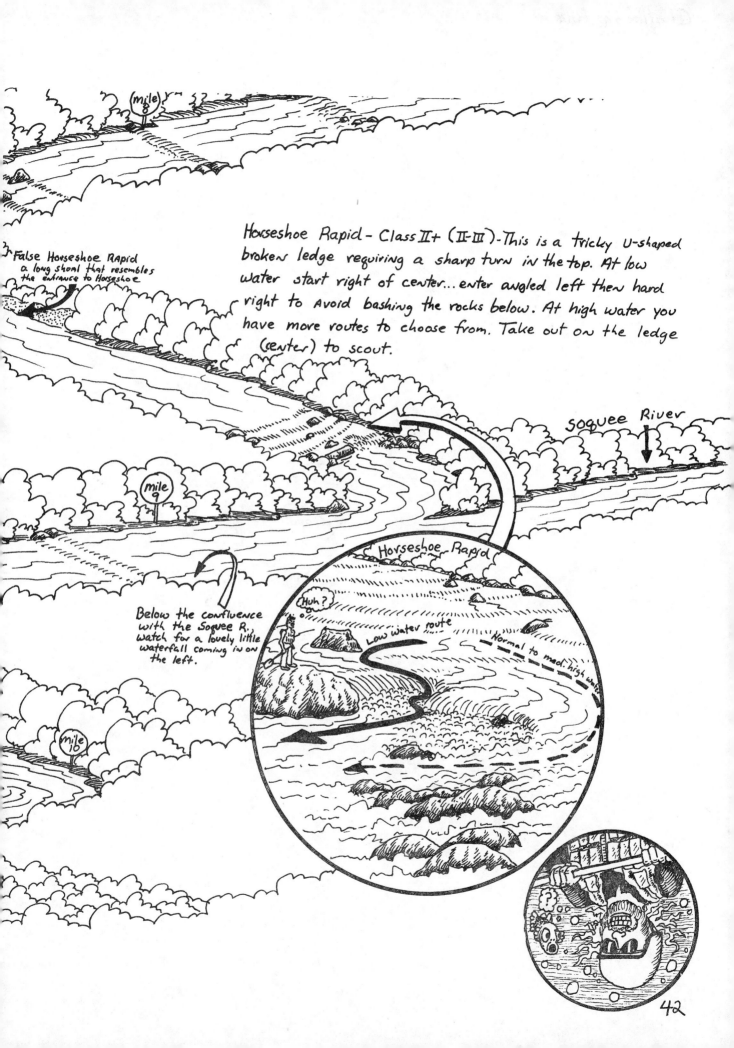

Horseshoe Rapid - Class II+ (II-III) - This is a tricky U-shaped broken ledge requiring a sharp turn in the top. At low water start right of center... enter angled left then hard right to Avoid bashing the rocks below. At high water you have more routes to choose from. Take out on the ledge (center) to scout.

False Horseshoe Rapid
a long shoal that resembles the entrance to Horseshoe

soquee River

mile 8

mile 9

mile 10

Below the confluence with the Soquee R. watch for a lovely little waterfall coming in on the left.

Horseshoe Rapid

Huh?

Low water route

Normal to med. high water

42

Chattooga River

CHATTOOGA

Chattooga River - Continued

The Chattooga is one of the most beautiful and exciting rivers in the United States. Included in the Wild & Scenic Rivers system in 1974, the Chattooga is protected from dams and development in perpetuity (Amen!). Flowing out of the mountains of Western N. Carolina, it forms a Natural border between Georgia and South Carolina. Scenes from the movie "Deliverance" were shot here, giving the Chattooga National fame and undeserved Noteriety [Actually, the river in the movie is a cinematic montage of the Chauga, Tallulah, and Chattooga]. The excellent water quality, unsurpassed scenery, and exciting rapids make this an extremely popular recreational river. There are Numerous professional outfitters in the area for those interested in a superlative outdoor experience.

Everyone boating or rafting down the river is required to register at the put in and comply with equipment guidelines & safety proceedures. These rules are enforced on the river and carry a very stiff fine for each violation!

Section Three offers 12.5 miles of fast water and Numerous rapids—(over a dozen Class III's & IV's and Bull Sluice, Class V). Skill levels required are intermediate to Advanced in open and decked boats. Section Three is to whitewater open-boating as the southside of Chicago is to R&B music — some of the S.E.'s most outstanding open boaters cut their whitewater teeth here.

Both sections are runnable year-round, with the best water levels occurring in Spring & early Summer.

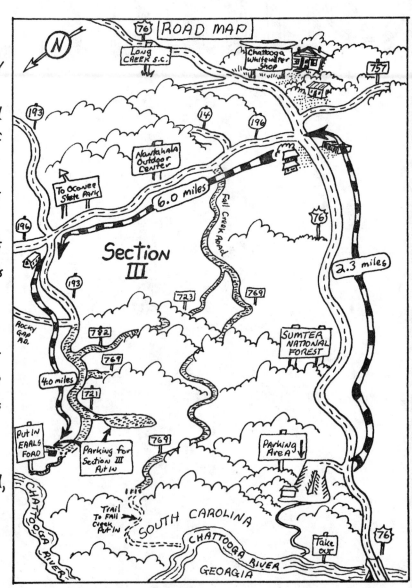

Section Four is the hard-core whitewater section, ornamented with some of the Southeast's toughest rapids. Skill levels required are advanced-intermediate to expert at or below a gauge reading of 1.8'. Above 1.8' this is "experts-only" whitewater — very pushy! In 1979, Sec. IV was run at over 5' by a group of true river-crazies — the river god was in a good mood THAT day!

In the last two years three boating fatalities have occurred here which point out some danger spots not usually mentioned. All occurred at relatively low water, all three victims were experienced on whitewater rivers (somewhat) and all had good support/rescue personnel on the scene when the fatal accidents occurred.

1. Fall, 1979 - a river guide was in the micro-eddy on the right, just above "Decapitation Rock" in Jawbone Rapid. His stern was swept under the rock and the kayak folded, trapping him underwater. Rescue was unsuccessful. Stay out of this eddy at any water level!

2. Fall, 1980 - An intermediate-level kayaker flipped in Corkscrew and tried to save her boat, declining several rescue ropes (one of which actually hit her). She was pulled into Left Crack of Crack-in-the-Rock and became lodged there. Despite immediate rescue and heroic resuscitation efforts, she died. This exact scenario occurred here several years ago with the same results. Do not go near Left Crack for any reason.

3. Spring 1981 - An experienced boater was running Bull Sluice in a tandem open boat. The water was so low the canoe got hung on the ledge above the upper hole. While trying to push the boat free with his foot he slipped and was swept left of Decap. Rock, where he became trapped in a crack or pothole (accounts of the accident differ here). Even though the water was low & rescue efforts began immediately, he drowned.

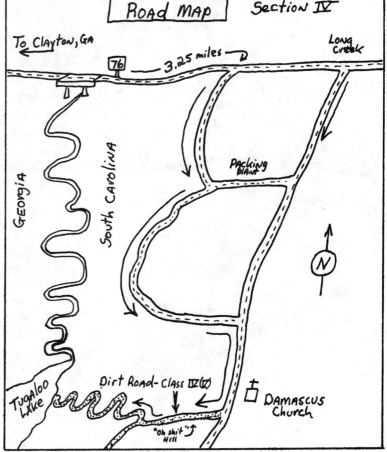

Road Map — Section IV

To Clayton, GA

76 — 3.25 miles →

Long Creek

Georgia

South Carolina

Packing Plant

N

Tugaloo Lake

Dirt Road - Class IV (V)

Damascus Church

"Oh shit" Hill

Chattooga River - Continued

WARWOMAN CREEK

mile 0

Put In: EARLS FORD

grunt!

Warwoman Rapids - Class III
Run first ledge Rt. of center. Run 2nd ledge far left angled to the right to miss the rocks below.

Rock Garden - If you saw "Deliverance" you'll recognize this - After a turn to the right it becomes a long technical rapid featuring tight chutes, ledges etc. Class II-III (III)

1st Island rapid - stay in the right channel and watch for log jams, particularly on the upstream end of the island.

mile 1

mile 2

Dicks Creek Ledge
mile 2.5

High water

SCOUTING ROCK

?

CUSHIONED ROCK

Dicks Creek ledge - Class IV
Scout from exposed rock rt. of center.
Run S-route angled to the right, brace into the cushioned rock, surf down, then left. Avoid going left of the cushioned rock! The 6' drop rt. of scouting rock can be run above 2.6' with discretion, as you can bust your bow or possibly pin vertically in it.

Dicks Creek FALLS

Run right of both Islands ½ mile below Dicks Creek Ledge

mile 3

SANDY FORD

ROCK CREEK

SECTION III

Facilities & Registration

SUMTER NATIONAL FOREST

NARROWS
mile 3.5

G

G

undercut rock

STONE CREEK

low Rock Garden, there are
eral Class II-III rapids until the
flat water above Dicks Creek.

The Narrows-Class IV
Half a mile below Sandy Ford
this long, intimidating rapid
begins...The top ¼ is a ledge-
staircase that chokes down to
a 25' slot with a violent wave in the
center. Run the top center, punch the wave
and eddy below. Set up throw ropes here to catch
bodies & boats. Sneak (or low water route) route goes far left
(broken line-diagram). It continues 150 yds. over class III drops
with a few offset holes to keep you guessing. The bottom drop
is on a blind turn to the right [you'll notice a cave-looking
formation on the left (S.C. side) Stay Away from the bottom left!
It's rocky, undercut, and usually stuffed with logs!] Run the bottom
drop starting rt. of center, then go far right to avoid the hole
by the undercut rock - Make the last half of the "S" and you're out.
This is a BAD place to swim! Half a mile below is 2nd ledge.

Top of Narrows -
see next page!

48

Chattooga River – Continued

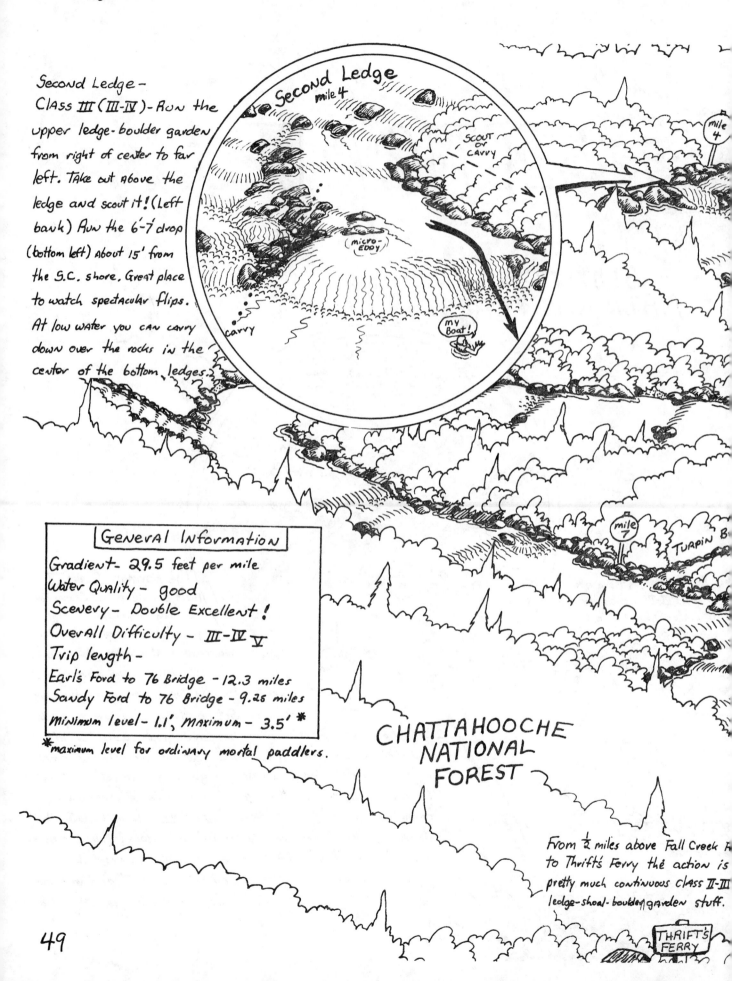

Second Ledge –
Class III (III-IV) – Run the upper ledge-boulder garden from right of center to far left. Take out above the ledge and scout it! (Left bank) Run the 6'-7' drop (bottom left) about 15' from the S.C. shore. Great place to watch spectacular flips.

At low water you can carry down over the rocks in the center of the bottom ledges.

(labels on illustration: Second Ledge mile 4 · SCOUT or CARRY · micro-EDDY · my Boat! · carry · mile 4 · mile 7 · TURPIN B)

General Information

Gradient – 29.5 feet per mile
Water Quality – good
Scenery – Double Excellent!
Overall Difficulty – III-IV V
Trip length –
Earl's Ford to 76 Bridge – 12.3 miles
Sandy Ford to 76 Bridge – 9.25 miles
Minimum level – 1.1', Maximum – 3.5' *

* maximum level for ordinary mortal paddlers.

CHATTAHOOCHE NATIONAL FOREST

From ½ miles above Fall Creek F to Thrift's Ferry the action is pretty much continuous class II-III ledge-shoal-boulder garden stuff.

THRIFT'S FERRY

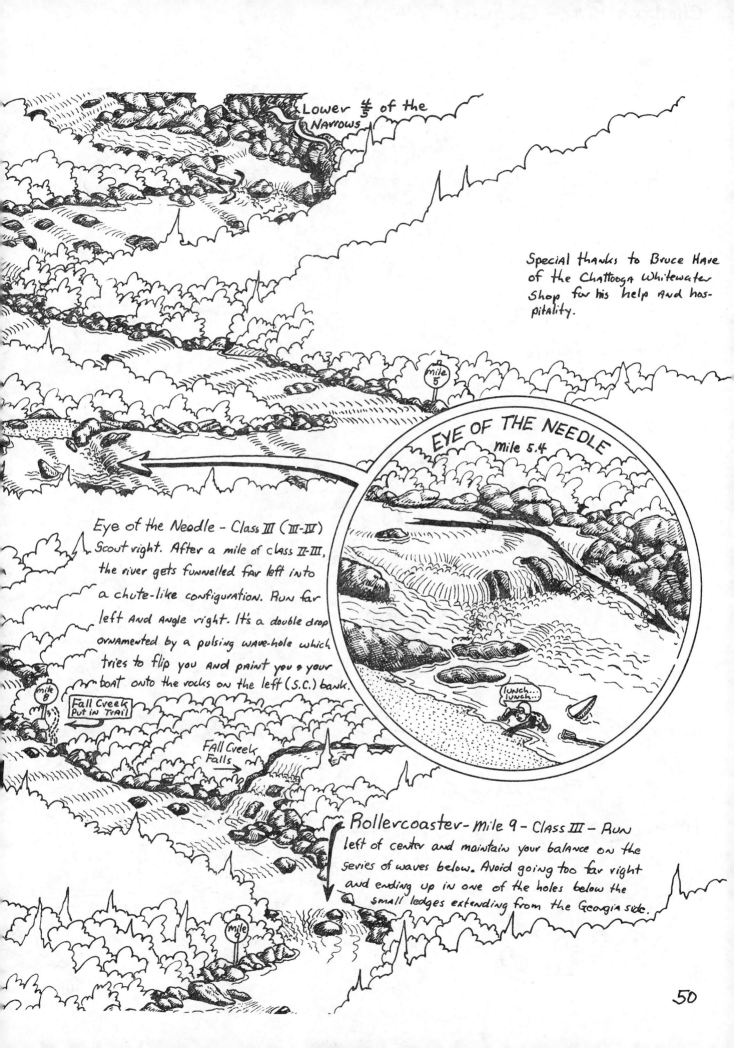

Lower 4/5 of the Narrows

Special thanks to Bruce Hare of the Chattooga Whitewater Shop for his help and hospitality.

mile 5

EYE OF THE NEEDLE
mile 5.4

lunch... lunch...

Eye of the Needle - Class III (III-IV) Scout right. After a mile of class II-III, the river gets funnelled far left into a chute-like configuration. Run far left and angle right. It's a double drop ornamented by a pulsing wave-hole which tries to flip you and paint you & your boat onto the rocks on the left (S.C.) bank.

mile 8

Fall Creek Put in Trail

Fall Creek Falls

Rollercoaster - Mile 9 - Class III - Run left of center and maintain your balance on the series of waves below. Avoid going too far right and ending up in one of the holes below the small ledges extending from the Georgia side.

mile

50

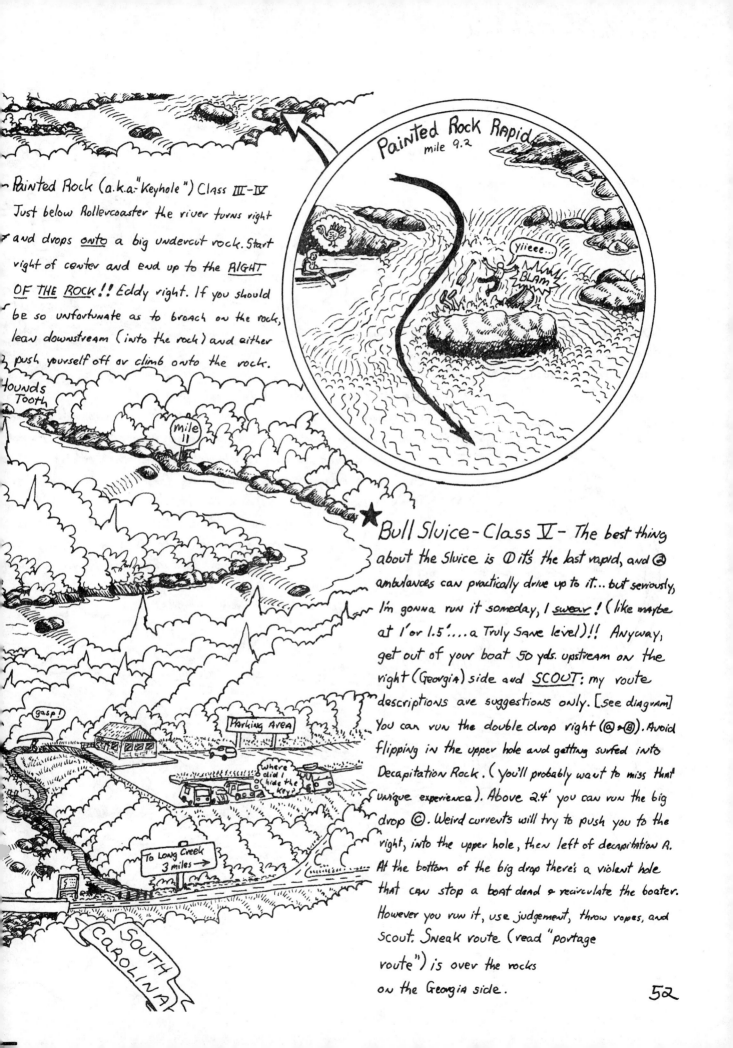

Painted Rock (a.k.a. "Keyhole") Class III-IV
Just below Rollercoaster the river turns right and drops onto a big undercut rock. Start right of center and end up to the RIGHT OF THE ROCK!! Eddy right. If you should be so unfortunate as to broach on the rock, lean downstream (into the rock) and either push yourself off or climb onto the rock.

Hounds Tooth

mile 11

Painted Rock Rapid
mile 9.2

yiieee...
BLAM

gasp!

Parking Area

where did I hide the key?

To Long Creek 3 miles →

SOUTH CAROLINA

★ Bull Sluice - Class V - The best thing about the Sluice is ① it's the last rapid, and ② ambulances can practically drive up to it... but seriously, I'm gonna run it someday, I swear! (like maybe at 1' or 1.5'....a Truly Sane level)!! Anyway, get out of your boat 50 yds. upstream on the right (Georgia) side and SCOUT: my route descriptions are suggestions only. [see diagram] You can run the double drop right (Ⓐ & Ⓑ). Avoid flipping in the upper hole and getting surfed into Decapitation Rock. (you'll probably want to miss that unique experience). Above 2.4' you can run the big drop Ⓒ. Weird currents will try to push you to the right, into the upper hole, then left of decapitation R. At the bottom of the big drop there's a violent hole that can stop a boat dead & recirculate the boater. However you run it, use judgement, throw ropes, and scout. Sneak route (read "portage route") is over the rocks on the Georgia side.

52

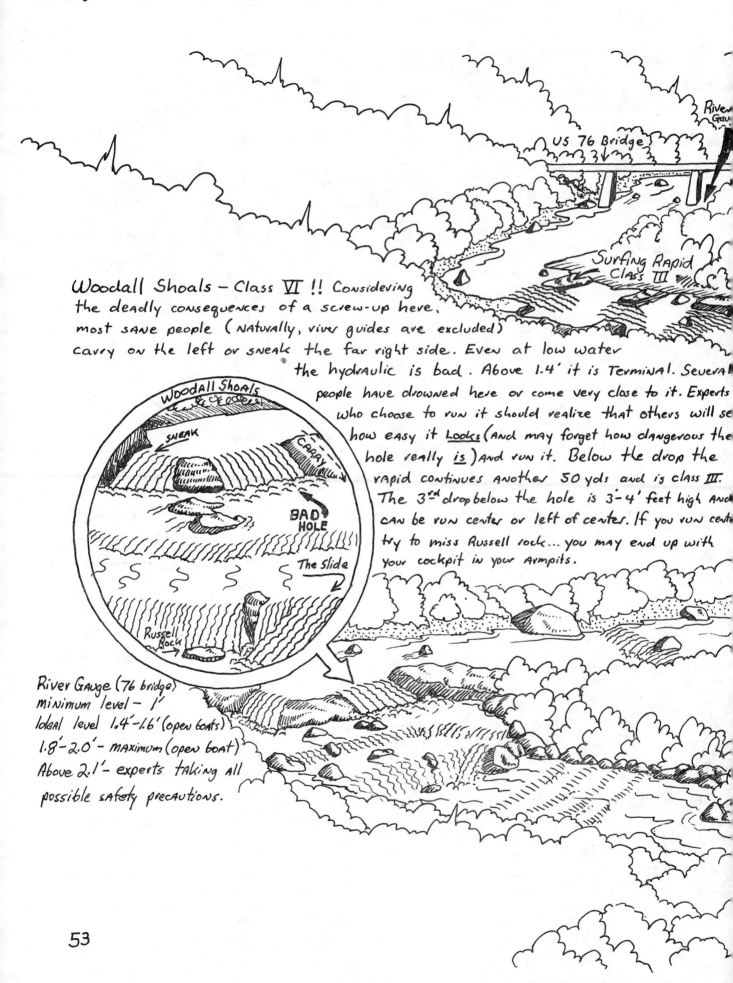

US 76 Bridge

River
Gau

Surfing Rapid
Class III

Woodall Shoals — Class VI !! Considering
the deadly consequences of a screw-up here,
most sane people (naturally, river guides are excluded)
carry on the left or sneak the far right side. Even at low water
the hydraulic is bad. Above 1.4' it is terminal. Several
people have drowned here or come very close to it. Experts
who choose to run it should realize that others will se
how easy it looks (and may forget how dangerous the
hole really is) and run it. Below the drop the
rapid continues another 50 yds and is class III.
The 3rd drop below the hole is 3'-4' feet high and
can be run center or left of center. If you run cente
try to miss Russell rock... you may end up with
your cockpit in your armpits.

Woodall Shoals

SNEAK

CARRY

BAD
HOLE

The Slide

Russell
Rock

River Gauge (76 bridge)
minimum level — 1'
Ideal level 1.4'-1.6' (open boats)
1.8'-2.0' — maximum (open boat)
Above 2.1' — experts taking all
possible safety precautions.

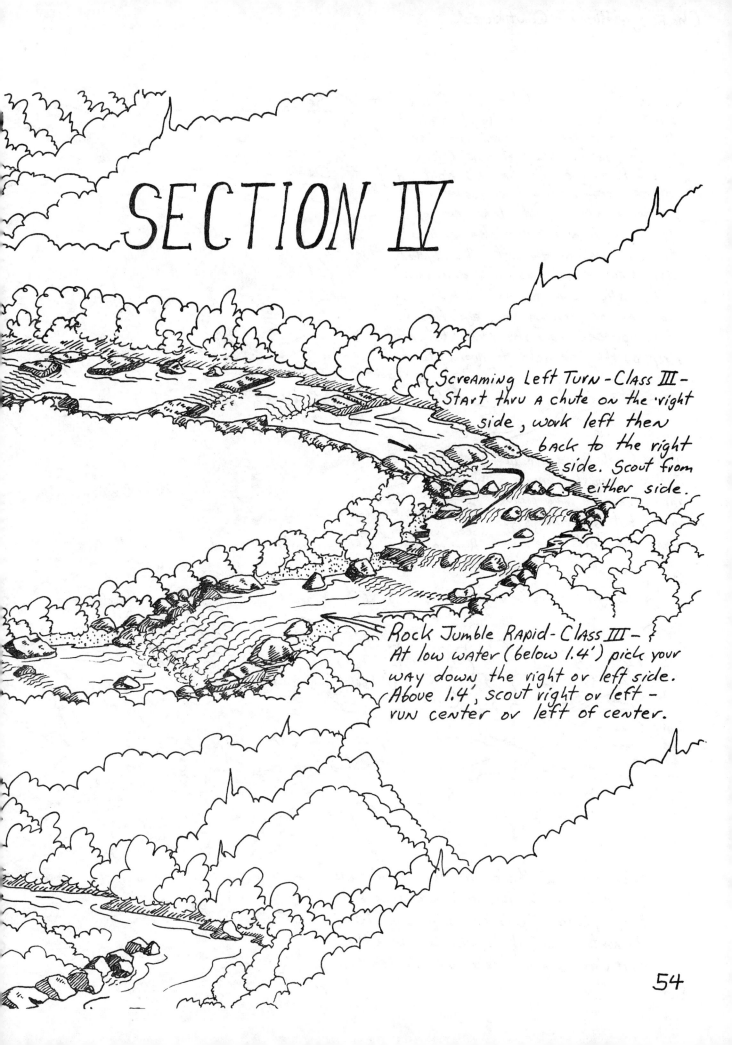

SECTION IV

Screaming Left Turn - Class III - Start thru a chute on the right side, work left then back to the right side. Scout from either side.

Rock Jumble Rapid - Class III - At low water (below 1.4') pick your way down the right or left side. Above 1.4', scout right or left - run center or left of center.

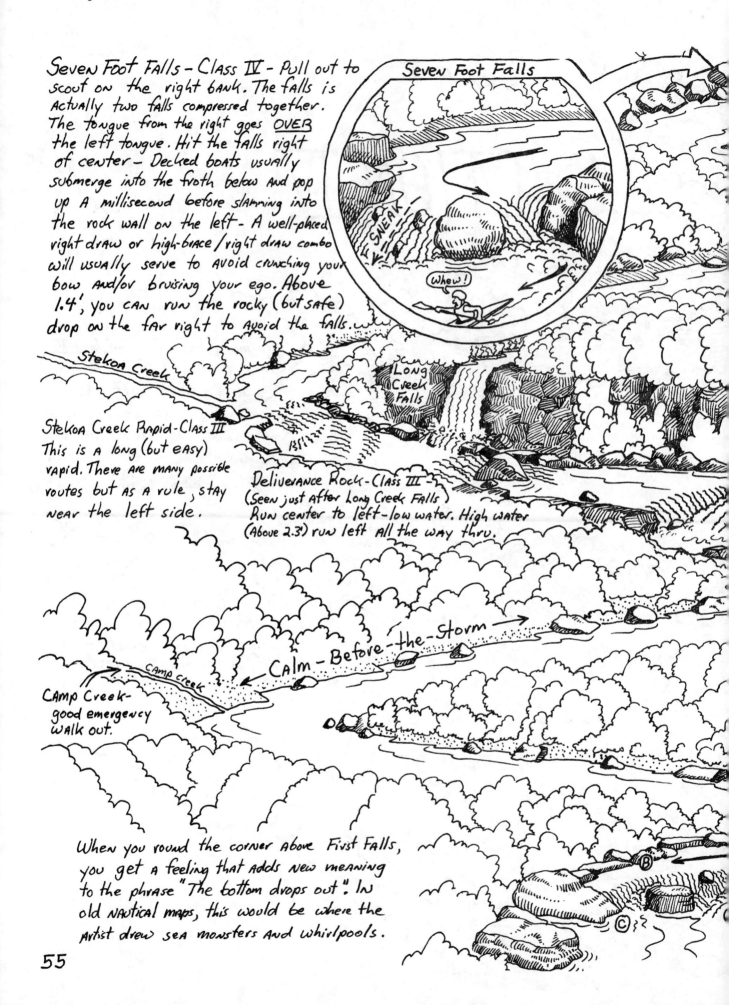

Seven Foot Falls - Class IV - Pull out to scout on the right bank. The falls is actually two falls compressed together. The tongue from the right goes OVER the left tongue. Hit the falls right of center - Decked boats usually submerge into the froth below and pop up a millisecond before slamming into the rock wall on the left - A well-placed right draw or high-brace/right draw combo will usually serve to avoid crunching your bow and/or bruising your ego. Above 1.4', you can run the rocky (but safe) drop on the far right to avoid the falls.

Stekoa Creek

Stekoa Creek Rapid - Class III This is a long (but easy) rapid. There are many possible routes but as a rule, stay near the left side.

Deliverance Rock - Class III - (Seen just after Long Creek Falls) Run center to left-low water. High water (above 2.3) run left all the way thru.

Long Creek Falls

Camp Creek- good emergency walk out.

Camp Creek

Calm - Before - the - Storm

When you round the corner above First Falls, you get a feeling that adds new meaning to the phrase "The bottom drops out". In old nautical maps, this would be where the artist drew sea monsters and whirlpools.

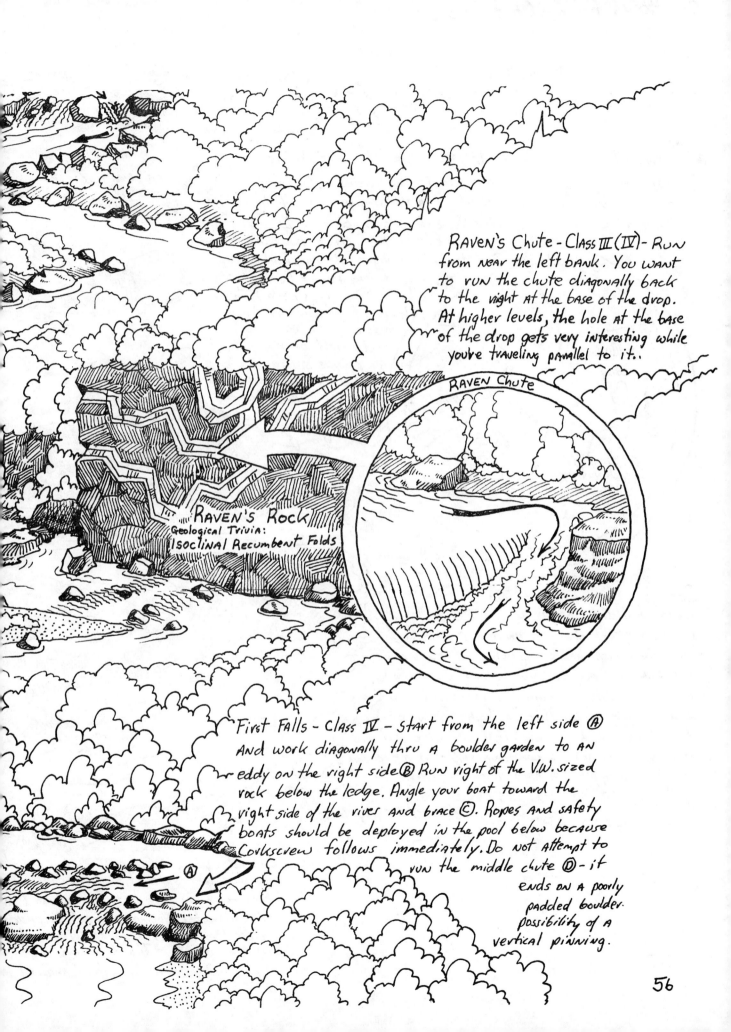

Raven's Chute - Class III (IV) - Run from near the left bank. You want to run the chute diagonally back to the right at the base of the drop. At higher levels, the hole at the base of the drop gets very interesting while you're traveling parallel to it..

RAVEN Chute

RAVEN'S ROCK
Geological Trivia:
Isoclinal Recumbent Folds

First Falls - Class IV - start from the left side Ⓐ and work diagonally thru a boulder garden to an eddy on the right side Ⓑ Run right of the V.W. sized rock below the ledge. Angle your boat toward the right side of the river and brace Ⓒ. Ropes and safety boats should be deployed in the pool below because Corkscrew follows immediately. Do not attempt to run the middle chute Ⓓ - it ends on a poorly padded boulder. possibility of a vertical pinning.

56

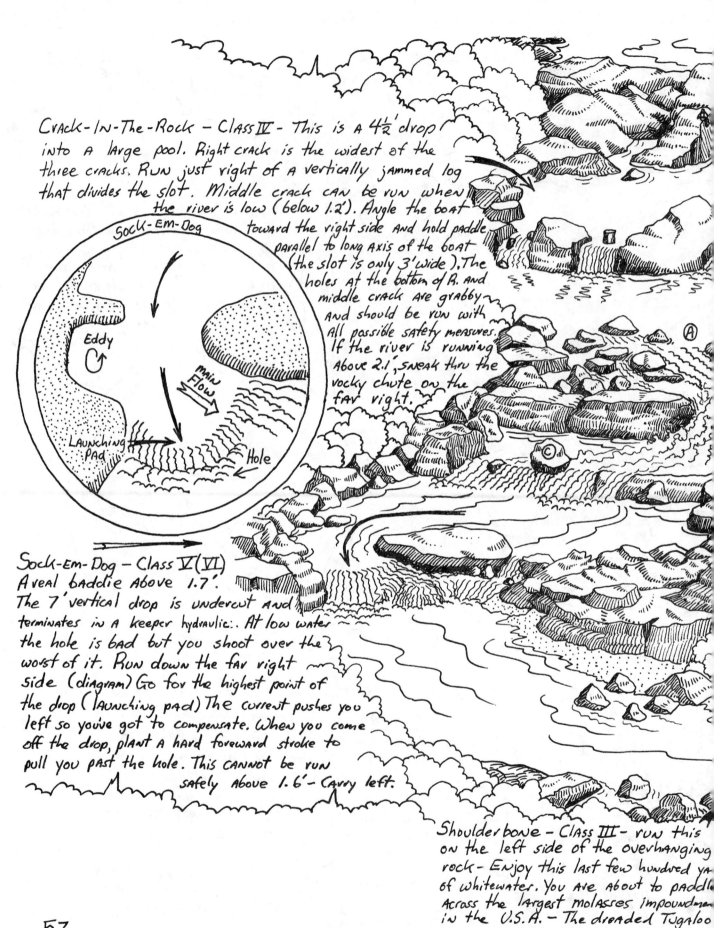

Crack-In-The-Rock — Class IV — This is a 4½' drop into a large pool. Right crack is the widest of the three cracks. Run just right of a vertically jammed log that divides the slot. Middle crack can be run when the river is low (below 1.2'). Angle the boat toward the right side and hold paddle parallel to long axis of the boat (the slot is only 3' wide). The holes at the bottom of R. and middle crack are grabby and should be run with all possible safety measures. If the river is running above 2.1', sneak thru the rocky chute on the far right.

Sock-Em-Dog

Eddy

Main Flow

Launching Pad

Hole

Sock-Em-Dog — Class V (VI)
A real baddie above 1.7'. The 7' vertical drop is undercut and terminates in a keeper hydraulic. At low water the hole is bad but you shoot over the worst of it. Run down the far right side (diagram) Go for the highest point of the drop (launching pad) The current pushes you left so you've got to compensate. When you come off the drop, plant a hard foreward stroke to pull you past the hole. This cannot be run safely above 1.6' — Carry left.

Shoulderbone — Class III — run this on the left side of the overhanging rock — Enjoy this last few hundred ya of whitewater. You are about to paddl across the largest molasses impoundme in the U.S.A. — The dreaded Tugaloo Lake — 2 miles of flatwater — Take out le

Corkscrew - Class IV(V) - Scout left or right (carry on the right). This is a difficult and violent plunge into some of the most bizzare water in the S.E.. Open boats generally swamp out. Decked boats tend to flip over and stay that way. Get out of your boat (right or left side) and SCOUT it! There's no way to accurately describe how to run it. Hint: Watch out for a nasty hole on the right just below the huge rock (usually decorated with spectators) at the bottom. This is the trickiest rapid on the river. Respect it! Again, ropes and safety boats MUST catch swimmers before they wash through Crack-In-the-Rock.

Danger !!

Jawbone - Class IV - scout from the left bank [Be sure to note Hydro-Electric Rock at the end of the first pool. This is no place to swim! People have been sucked thru holes in the base of the rock] Start from the right Ⓐ Run down the center. You can catch an upper eddy on the left Ⓑ Stay to the left of Hydroelectric Ⓒ pull out on the left-Sock-em-Dog is just below

Ⓑ

Rapid ratings in parenthesis (ex: Class III (IV)) indicate a change in difficulty at higher levels. Above 2.0', for example, Corkscrew, the Dog, etc. get exponentially harder.

Thanks and a tip of the yak to:
Henry Unger and Dave Plott
for their advice and guidance
and, of course, Holly and Donna!

58

Cheat Canyon

Cheat
River

West
Virginia

CHEAT CANYON

Revised Post-Flood Edition!

Cheat Canyon – continued

After the Flood...

ON November 5, 1985 torrential rains triggered by Hurricane Juan swelled the Cheat to 230,000 c.f.s. (at crest)! The floodwaters swept away several towns (including a goodly portion of Albright) and then dynamically remodelled much of Cheat Canyon. When the floodwaters receded 38 people were dead, 2500 were homeless and damage was in the millions.

The good news is we got ourselves a new river. From a boater's perspective the major flood-wrought changes occurred at Beech Run Rapids, Big Nasty, and Coliseum. Additionally, floodwaters scoured thirty feet up the banks on both sides of the river, rolled house-sized mega-boulders around like ping pong balls, carved new channels in the old riverbed and rearranged all those nice rounded river rocks & boulders into Nature's equivalent of "shot rock". Watch out for lots of sharp, upstream-pointing rocks in the river! Swimmers beware, particularly at Coliseum just below Cyclotron. Remember, this is a geologically "new" river so scout the unfamiliar stuff and expect the unexpected...

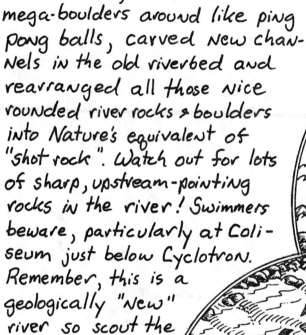

Coliseum (before flood*)

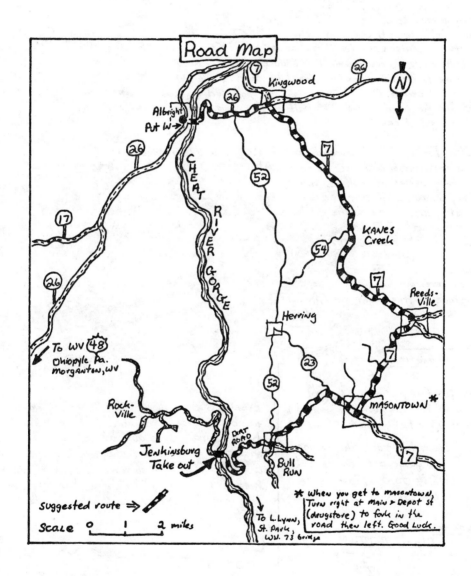

Road Map

N

26
Kingwood

7

26
Albright
Put In →

CHEAT RIVER GORGE

26

7

52

17

KANES
Creek

26

54

7

Reeds-
Ville

Herring

To WV 48
Ohiopyle Pa.
Morganton, WV

23

7

52

MASONTOWN *

Rock-
Ville

DIRT ROAD

7

Jenkinsburg
Take out →

Bull
Run

* When you get to Masontown,
turn right at Main & Depot St
(drugstore) to fork in the
road then left. Good luck.

suggested route ⇒

SCALE 0   1   2 miles

To L. Lynn,
St. Park,
WV. 73 bridge

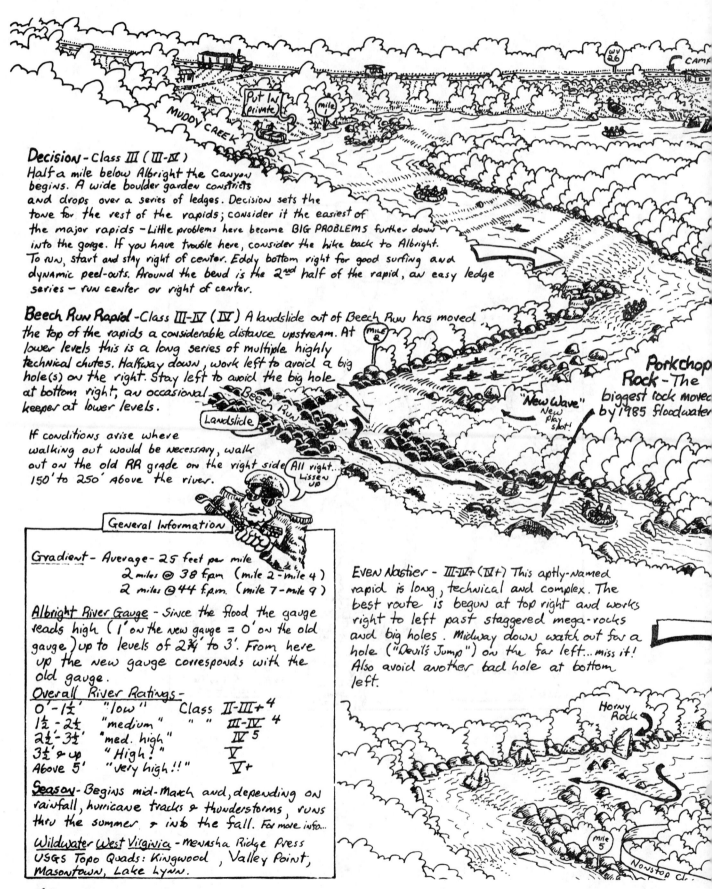

Decision - Class III (II-IV)
Half a mile below Albright the Canyon begins. A wide boulder garden constricts and drops over a series of ledges. Decision sets the tone for the rest of the rapids; consider it the easiest of the major rapids – Little problems here become BIG PROBLEMS further down into the gorge. If you have trouble here, consider the hike back to Albright. To run, start and stay right of center. Eddy bottom right for good surfing and dynamic peel-outs. Around the bend is the 2nd half of the rapid, an easy ledge series – run center or right of center.

Beech Run Rapid - Class III-IV (IV)
A landslide out of Beech Run has moved the top of the rapids a considerable distance upstream. At lower levels this is a long series of multiple highly technical chutes. Halfway down, work left to avoid a big hole(s) on the right. Stay left to avoid the big hole at bottom right, an occasional keeper at lower levels.

If conditions arise where walking out would be necessary, walk out on the old RR grade on the right side 150' to 250' above the river.

General Information

Gradient - Average - 25 feet per mile
2 miles @ 38 f.p.m. (mile 2 - mile 4)
2 miles @ 44 f.p.m. (mile 7 - mile 9)

Albright River Gauge - Since the flood the gauge reads high (1' on the new gauge = 0' on the old gauge) up to levels of 2¾' to 3'. From here up the new gauge corresponds with the old gauge.

Overall River Ratings -

0' - 1½'	"low"	Class II-III+	4
1½ - 2½'	"medium"	" " II-IV	4
2½' - 3½'	"med. high"	IV	5
3½' & up	"High!"	V	
Above 5'	"very high!!"	V+	

Season - Begins mid-March and, depending on rainfall, hurricane tracks & thunderstorms, runs thru the summer & into the fall. For more info...

Wildwater West Virginia - Menasha Ridge Press
USGS Topo Quads: Kingwood, Valley Point, Masontown, Lake Lynn.

Even Nastier - III-IV+ (IV+)
This aptly-named rapid is long, technical and complex. The best route is begun at top right and works right to left past staggered mega-rocks and big holes. Midway down watch out for a hole ("Devil's Jump") on the far left... miss it! Also avoid another bad hole at bottom left.

Porkchop Rock - The biggest rock moved by 1985 floodwater

"New Wave" New play spot!

All right... Lissen up

Landslide

Horny Rock

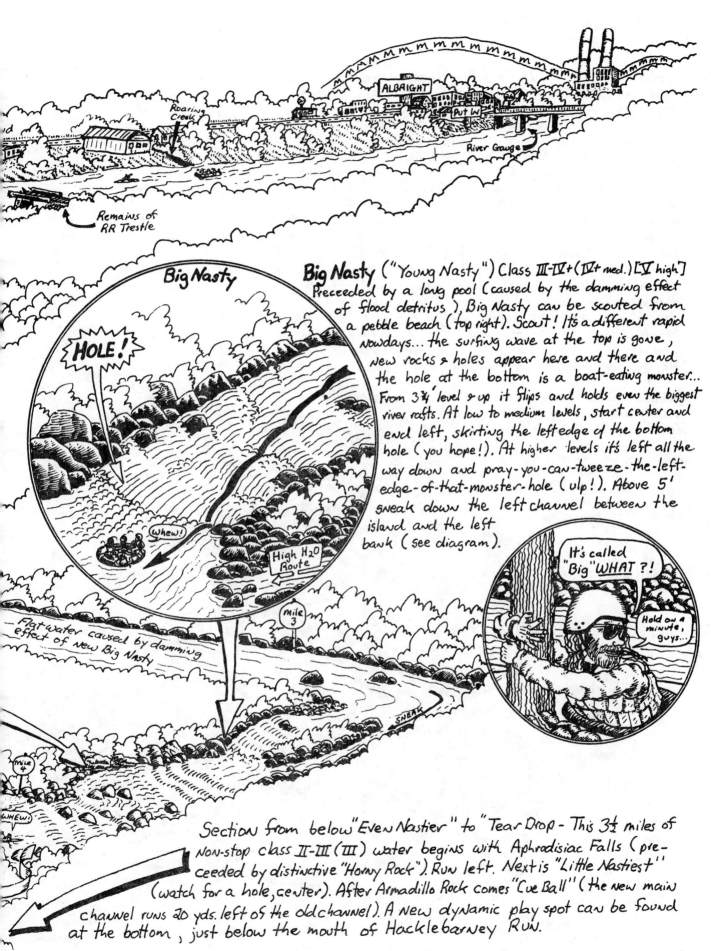

Big Nasty ("Young Nasty") Class III-IV+ (IV+ med.) [V high] Preceeded by a long pool (caused by the damming effect of flood detritus), Big Nasty can be scouted from a pebble beach (top right). Scout! It's a different rapid nowdays... the surfing wave at the top is gone, new rocks & holes appear here and there and the hole at the bottom is a boat-eating monster... From 3¾' level & up it flips and holds even the biggest river rafts. At low to medium levels, start center and end left, skirting the left edge of the bottom hole (you hope!). At higher levels it's left all the way down and pray-you-can-tweeze-the-left-edge-of-that-monster-hole (ulp!). Above 5' sneak down the left channel between the island and the left bank (see diagram).

Section from below "Even Nastier" to "Tear Drop" - This 3½ miles of non-stop class II-III (III) water begins with Aphrodisiac Falls (preceeded by distinctive "Horny Rock"). Run left. Next is "Little Nastiest" (watch for a hole, center). After Armadillo Rock comes "Cue Ball" (the new main channel runs 20 yds. left of the old channel). A new dynamic play spot can be found at the bottom, just below the mouth of Hacklebarney Run.

Cheat Canyon, cont'd.

Coliseum - IV+ (V) [V+] - The most dramatically flood-changed rapid on the Cheat! The main channel which used to run down the left now plunges down the right side of the riverbed in a series of drops, holes, and reaction pillows known collectively as "Cyclotron" (diagram (A)). Signalled by a prominent square mega-rock at top left, the first big drop ("Recyclotron") is a big riverwide hole with a clean chute on the right (which widens as water levels rise) and a good safety rock below. Run the right chute and avoid a second hole just below on the left. 10 to 15 yards below is the "Particle Accelerator", a diagonal reaction pillow that kicks to the right into a mega-hole ("Cloud Chamber") just below. At lower levels aim for the pyramidical rock creating the pillow for maximum thrills. At higher levels, sneak the whole thing on a wide tongue on the right. From the big pool at the bottom work far left and skirt "Devil's Trap" * (diagram, (B)) on the left and continue to pass left of "Pillow Rock" ((C)) and left of Picture Rock ((D)) below. The flood deposited a coal truck-sized rock behind Picture Rock creating a tight, dangerous chute. An alternate route from the pool below Cyclotron to the top of "Pete Morgan" would be to work your way thru a technical boulder garden ' ending right of Pillow Rock ((C)). Avoid the "deadend chute" leading off center from Cyclotron's bottom pool (see diagram) because of its numerous pinning possibilities. At high water run far left (diagram, bow arrow).

*Additional Info - Watch out for a nasty pinning rock in the hole at Devil's Trap (B), right of center. From the bottom of Devil's Trap at or below 2½', the optimal route (white arrow) runs to the right of Pillow Rock ((C)) then back to the left to set up for "Pete Morgan", just below.

' Boulder Garden Route, dotted line; decked boats only... tight!

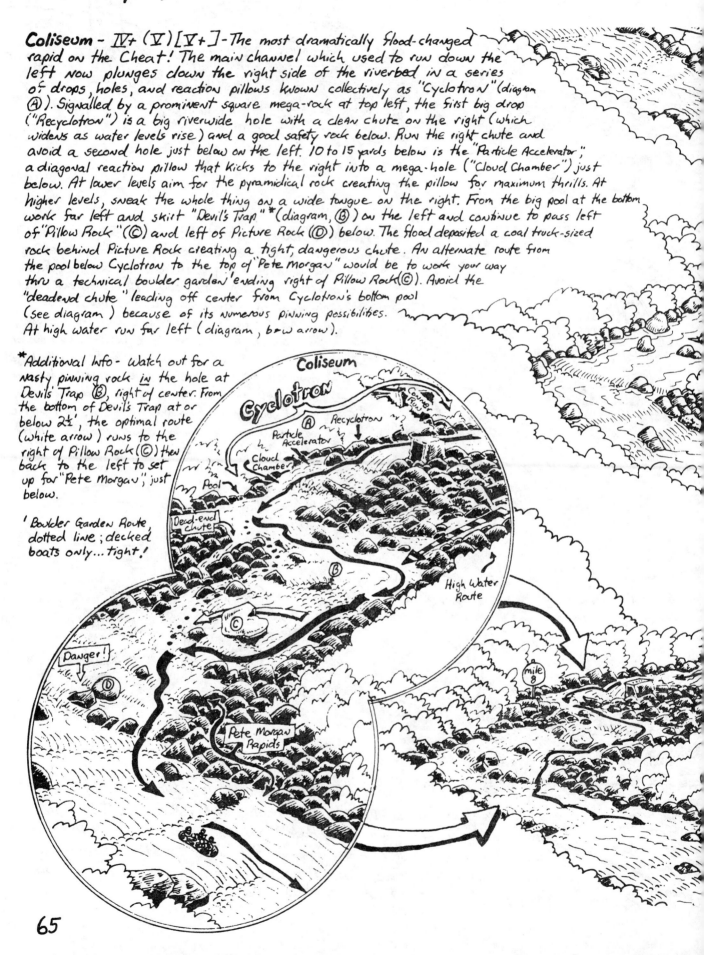

65

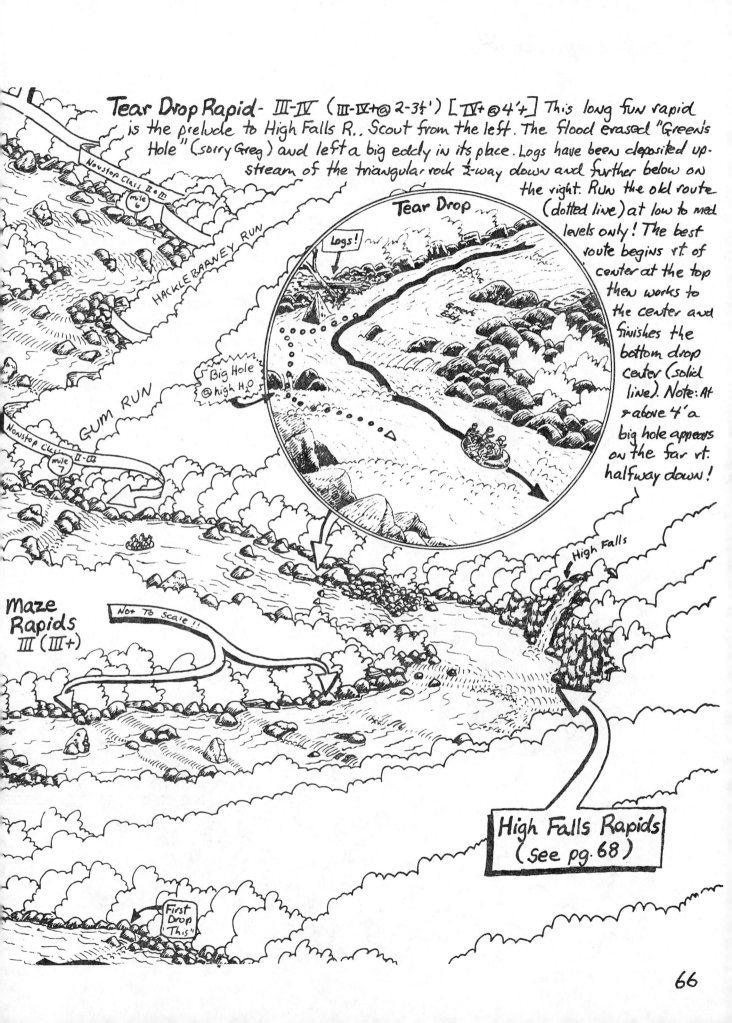

Tear Drop Rapid - III-IV (III-IV+ @ 2-3½') [IV+ @ 4'+] This long fun rapid is the prelude to High Falls R.. Scout from the left. The flood erased "Green's Hole" (sorry Greg) and left a big eddy in its place. Logs have been deposited upstream of the triangular rock ½-way down and further below on the right. Run the old route (dotted line) at low to med levels only! The best route begins rt. of center at the top then works to the center and finishes the bottom drop center (solid line). Note: At & above 4' a big hole appears on the far rt. halfway down!

Tear Drop

Logs!

Green's eddy

Big Hole @ high H₂O

Nonstop Class II & III
mile 6

HACKLE BARNEY RUN

GUM RUN

Nonstop Class II-III
mile 7

High Falls

Maze Rapids III (III+)

Not To Scale!!

High Falls Rapids (see pg. 68)

First Drop "This"

Cheat Canyon, cont'd.

"**This, That, What?! Rapids**" (A.K.A. "Boulderline")
Class III + (IV) Alas, the ender hole is gone... Anyhow,
after the big pool below Coliseum you encounter a
long rapid with three distinct drops; This, That and
What. First Drop ("This") - Start center & cut left into a
series of standing waves. Eddy on the right in the pool
below. Second Drop ("That") - run center, move to the
right then cut back to the left. Third Drop ("What?!") -
here you want to aim for the left side of a prominent
square rock while simultaneously avoiding a hole/trap
on the far left. From here, move back to the right and
end up center at the bottom. At high water (4'& up)
keep right of the big rock above the final drop (dotted line, above rt.).

really....

GREAT HOLE HUH?

Yiieeeee

OMYGOD!!

TAKE
OUT

Big Sandy
Creek

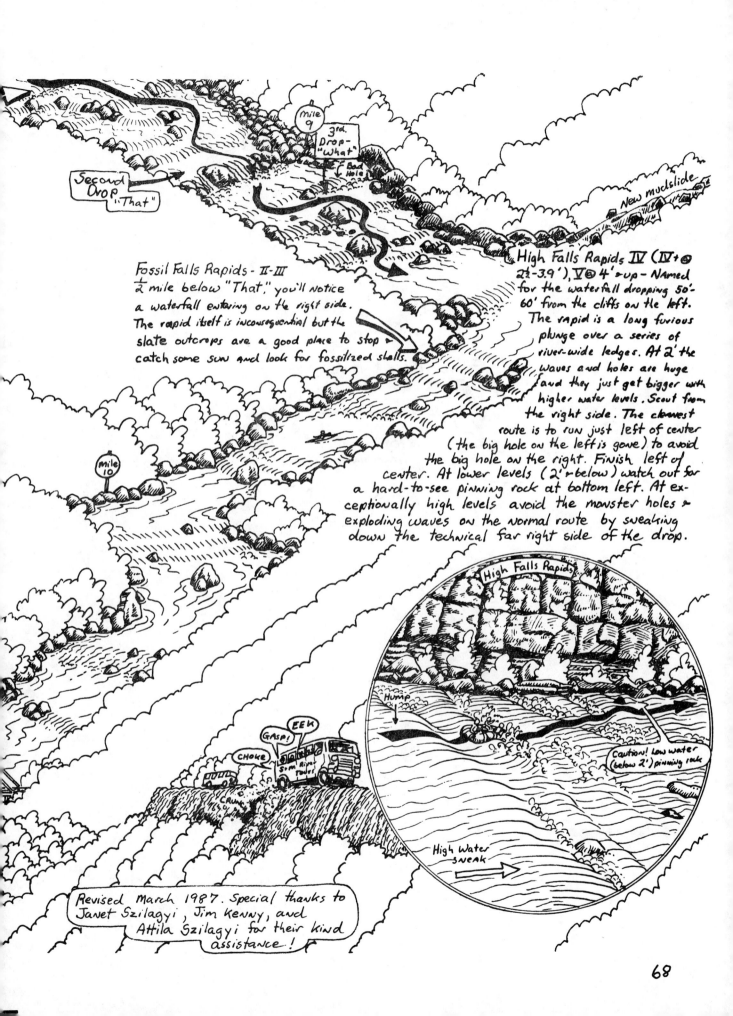

mile 9

3rd. Drop "What"

Bad Hole

Second Drop "That"

New mudslide

Fossil Falls Rapids - II-III
½ mile below "That," you'll notice a waterfall entering on the right side. The rapid itself is inconsequential but the slate outcrops are a good place to stop & catch some sun and look for fossilized shells.

mile 10

High Falls Rapids IV (IV+ @ 2½-3.9'), V @ 4' & up - Named for the waterfall dropping 50'-60' from the cliffs on the left. The rapid is a long furious plunge over a series of river-wide ledges. At 2' the waves and holes are huge & they just get bigger with higher water levels. Scout from the right side. The cleanest route is to run just left of center (the big hole on the left is gone) to avoid the big hole on the right. Finish left of center. At lower levels (2' & below) watch out for a hard-to-see pinning rock at bottom left. At exceptionally high levels avoid the monster holes & exploding waves on the normal route by sneaking down the technical far right side of the drop.

High Falls Rapids

Hump

Caution! Low water (below 2') pinning rock

High Water Sneak

EEK
GASP!
CHOKE
Sun River Tours

Revised March 1987. Special thanks to Janet Szilagyi, Jim Kenny, and Attila Szilagyi for their kind assistance!

68

French Broad River

French Broad River

North
Carolina

FRENCH BROAD & BIG LAUREL

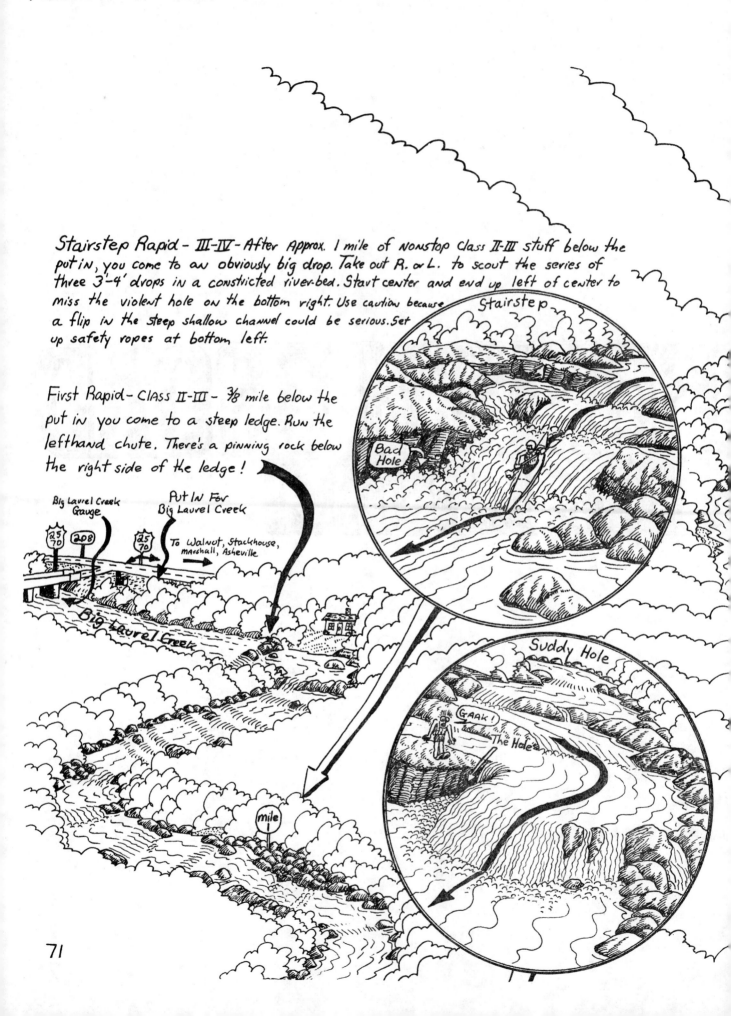

Stairstep Rapid - III-IV - After Approx. 1 mile of nonstop Class II-III stuff below the put in, you come to an obviously big drop. Take out R. or L. to scout the series of three 3'-4' drops in a constricted river-bed. Start center and end up left of center to miss the violent hole on the bottom right. Use caution because a flip in the steep shallow channel could be serious. Set up safety ropes at bottom left.

First Rapid - CLASS II-III - 3/8 mile below the put in you come to a steep ledge. Run the lefthand chute. There's a pinning rock below the right side of the ledge !

Big Laurel Creek Gauge

Put In For Big Laurel Creek

25 70   208   25 70

To Walnut, Stackhouse, Marshall, Asheville

Big Laurel Creek

Stairstep

Bad Hole

Suddy Hole

GAAK !

The Hole

mile

Barnard

Put In
River gauge

Beginner's Rapid

French Broad

Maze Rapid
II-III (III)

mile

Big Pillow Rapid

No Name Rapid
II-III

mile 3

Wesley's Rock

Big Pillow Rapid - Class III+ (III-IV)
Take out on the beach on the left to scout. The riverbed gets very obstructed and the course takes you left thru a long boulder-ledge series. Pick your way down and take the obvious chute over a 3' drop & into a hole. Stay to your right to miss the pillow rock ("Wesley's Rock"). There is a small chute just left of Wesley's rock if you screw up seriously. Run the ledges below on the left or far right at low water.

French Broad – Continued

Suddy Hole – Class III+
A distinct horizon line and g... below signal you to pull over on... right to scout the drop. The hole is... the far right; a 4' drop into a 3-4' wide crevas... Leave the hole to the real crazies – it's a very bad place to... stuck in! Run the slanting rocky drop just left... center on the obvious tongue. Even at 1', you... a scrape, so glass boats may want t... at low levels. There... recovery pool at the...

An old logging road runs the length of Big Laurel on the left side. Use for scouting & emergency exit!

Ruins Loggin... Ru...

Narrows – Class IV (IV-V) ⅓ miles below Suddy Hole the river turns right and an island divides the current. Run L. or rt. of the island. Just below, the river gets squeezed against a rock bluff on the right... run right. Below is a quartermile of nonstop 80' per mile Class III-IV rapids with a dangerous Class IV at the bottom! In general, stay center & watch out for a big powerful hole ⅜ of the way down. After a brief slack section, the river bends left and the bottom drops out. Eddy on the rock outcrops on the right to scout. The bottom rapid starts with a 3' drop onto a 60' long slanting shelf of rock. The whole channel is funnelled down into a violent hole at the bottom. Run by starting far right for the 3' drop, then either right of center or left of center for the steep shallow shelf. A flip and swim at the top is potentially serious because of the shallowness of the water and the velocity of the current. This can also be run from the far left but the first drop requires a fast turn to avoid a pinning situation – not recommended! Good recovery pool at the bottom.

Last Rapid – Narrows – Class IV

Omygoo!

Big Lau...

Very Special Than... Brad Howarth, Hen... Unger, Sue, Smoky... River Expeditions, And Schlinkert for their assistance making this map!

Note: the portage route on the right is 5.6 – bring your E.B.'s!

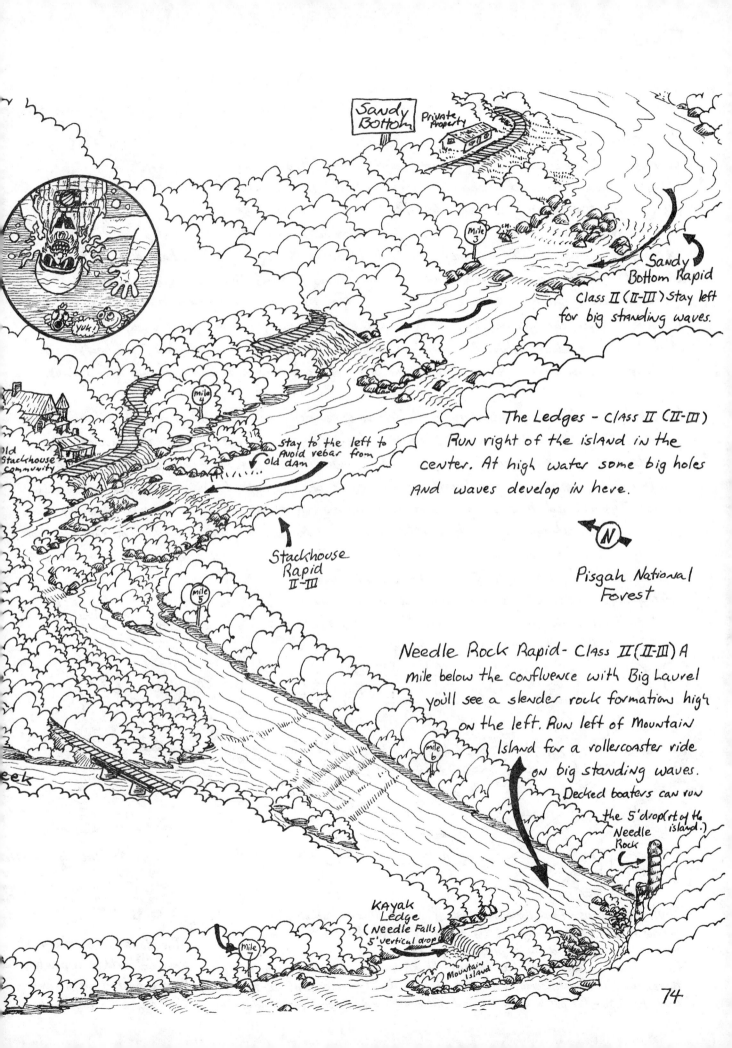

Sandy Bottom

Private Property

Mile 3

Sandy Bottom Rapid
Class II (II-III) Stay left
for big standing waves.

Mile 4

Old Stackhouse Community

Stay to the left to
Avoid rebar from
Old dam

The Ledges - CLASS II (II-III)
Run right of the island in the
center. At high water some big holes
And waves develop in here.

(N) Pisgah National
Forest

Stackhouse
Rapid
II-III

mile 5

yuk!

eek

Needle Rock Rapid- Class II (II-III) A
mile below the confluence with Big Laurel
you'll see a slender rock formation high
on the left. Run left of Mountain
Island for a rollercoaster ride
on big standing waves.
Decked boaters can run

the 5' drop (rt of the island.)
Needle
Rock

mile 6

Kayak
Ledge
(Needle Falls)
5' vertical drop

mile 7

Mountain Island

French Broad - Continued

Big Laurel Creek - This outstanding whitewater run should NOT be missed, if you can catch it with good water! Big Laurel plunges through a wild & beautiful demi-gorge, with mountains rising 1000 feet above on both sides. The gradient averages 50-60 f.p.m. with the Narrows section dropping at 80 f.p.m.! The action is pretty much non-stop drop-pool rapids with several major drops that should be scouted. Intermediate & advanced decked & open boaters should have no serious problems here <u>at normal water levels</u>. Scouting and safety ropes are mandatory! The minimum level for a "good run" is 6" above 0" (you can get down it at 6" below 0", but it's "bang! scrape!!" all the way. A reading of 1' to 1.5' is ideal. Above 2' things get pushy but it's runnable if you're good. The best time to run is Spring & early Summer - Runoff is fast & the creek drops to unrunnable levels in only a few days.

French Broad - This is a BIG river with lots of whitewater action, even when the river is low. The gradient averages 29 feet per mile with many rapids of the ledge-shoal variety. There are several major rapids that will need scouting, particularly Deep Water Rapid (aka "Frank Bell's Rapid) at mile 7.6. The Southern RR tracks run the length of the river on the right for scouting and emergency access. The RR bed runs along what used to be an old stagecoach road between Asheville and Hot Springs. Downstream of the hwy. 25/70 bridge in Hot Springs are the ruins of the old Hot Springs Resort. The ruins and hot springs are on private property, so get permission before exploring. For overnight stays, the Rocky Bluff Campground (outside Hot Springs on Rt. 209) is recommended. For water levels call Smoky Mtn. River Expeditions or TVA ((604)637-0101, Ext. 2054) and request the Newport Gauge reading.

Shuttle directions - From Hot Springs, take 25/70 west toward Asheville. When you get to Walnut take a right at the top of the hill (at the gas station & old church). 1.3 miles down a precipitous paved road puts you in Barnard. Turn left onto a dirt road after crossing the RR tracks and Voila... you're there. For Big Laurel: same route but stop at the T-junction of 25-70 75 and Rt 208 - The put in is on the East side of the bridge below the parking area.

* Beer is available at the Tennessee/N St. line. From Hot Springs head East on 25 for approximately 9 miles.

★ The take out, on the right above 25/70 bridge is privately owned. Private boaters are allowed to use it - please be considerate.

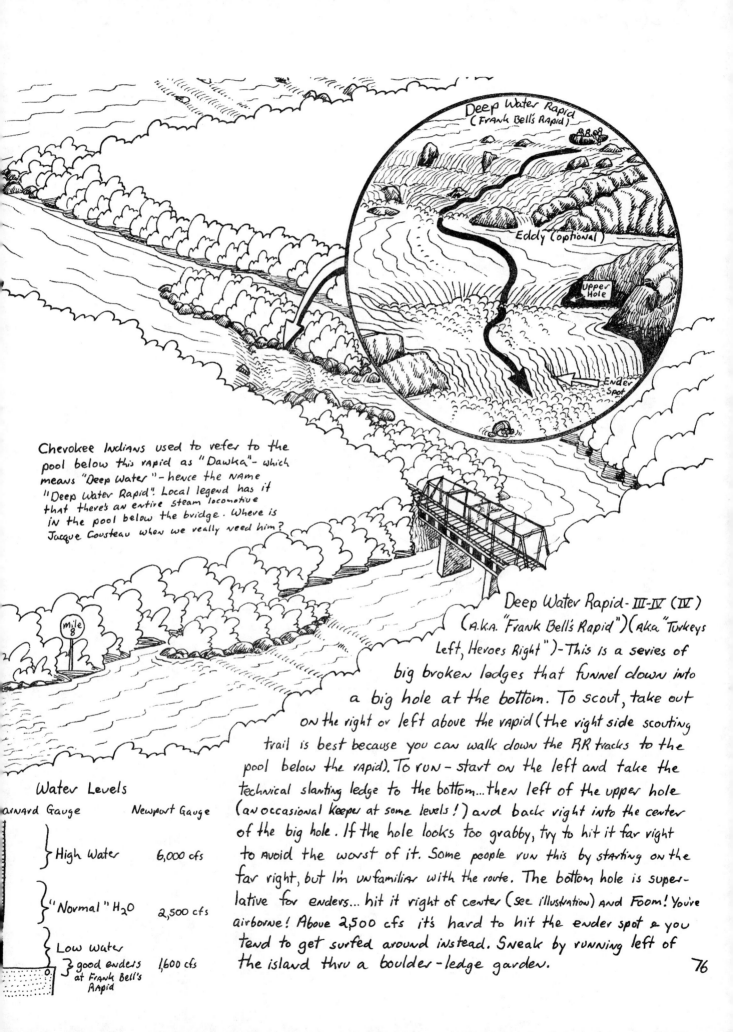

Deep Water Rapid
(Frank Bell's Rapid)

Eddy (optional)

Upper Hole

Ender Spot

Chevokee Indians used to refer to the pool below this rapid as "Dawka" - which means "Deep Water" - hence the name "Deep Water Rapid". Local legend has it that there's an entire steam locomotive in the pool below the bridge. Where is Jacque Cousteau when we really need him?

mile 8

Deep Water Rapid- III-IV (IV)
(a.k.a. "Frank Bell's Rapid")(aka "Turkeys Left, Heroes Right")-This is a series of big broken ledges that funnel down into a big hole at the bottom. To scout, take out on the right or left above the rapid (the right side scouting trail is best because you can walk down the RR tracks to the pool below the rapid). To run - start on the left and take the technical slanting ledge to the bottom...then left of the upper hole (an occasional keeper at some levels!) and back right into the center of the big hole. If the hole looks too grabby, try to hit it far right to avoid the worst of it. Some people run this by starting on the far right, but I'm unfamiliar with the route. The bottom hole is superlative for enders... hit it right of center (see illustration) and Foom! You're airborne! Above 2,500 cfs it's hard to hit the ender spot & you tend to get surfed around instead. Sneak by running left of the island thru a boulder-ledge garden.

Water Levels

Barnard Gauge	Newport Gauge
High Water	6,000 cfs
"Normal" H₂O	2,500 cfs
Low water	
good enders at Frank Bell's Rapid	1,600 cfs

76

Gauley River

West Virginia

Gauley River

THE GAULEY

Gauley River – Continued

The Gauley can be a whitewater heaven or a whitewater hell, depending on your ability, the water level, and the weather. Below Summersville Dam the river cuts a deep canyon thru a remote mountainous area. Plenty rivers are steeper and higher volume, but the Gauley stands out as the classic big water run in the East. The run is so challenging that the area's river outfitters require that even their customers have prior whitewater experience! This is a run for advanced-intermediate to expert boaters only. If you don't have a dependable roll or self-rescue (open boats), don't do it. A swim through even the small rapids is very dangerous because of radical undercutting of boulders and sandstone formations. Swimming any one of the major rapids is bad indeed. There are over 100 rapids in 26 miles of river, with ten rapids in the Class IV to V catagory. "Normal" water is 2,200-2,800 3,500 cfs is considered medium-high. The Gauley can be run as low as 950 cfs — it's technical

Sweets Falls   Henry Unger Photo

tight, and plenty challenging...plus you get to see how undercut the rocks really are.

Overall River Ratings –
900 cfs – 1500 cfs – Class III-IV IV
1600 – 2,100 cfs – Class IV V
2,200 – 3,500 cfs – Class IV-V VI
The highest the Gauley has been run (to my knowledge) is 8,500 cfs!

Releases occur in September and October on a scheduled basis. During particularly wet summers there are unscheduled low water releases (from 900-2,000 cfs). Check it if you're in the area.

Gauley River - Continued

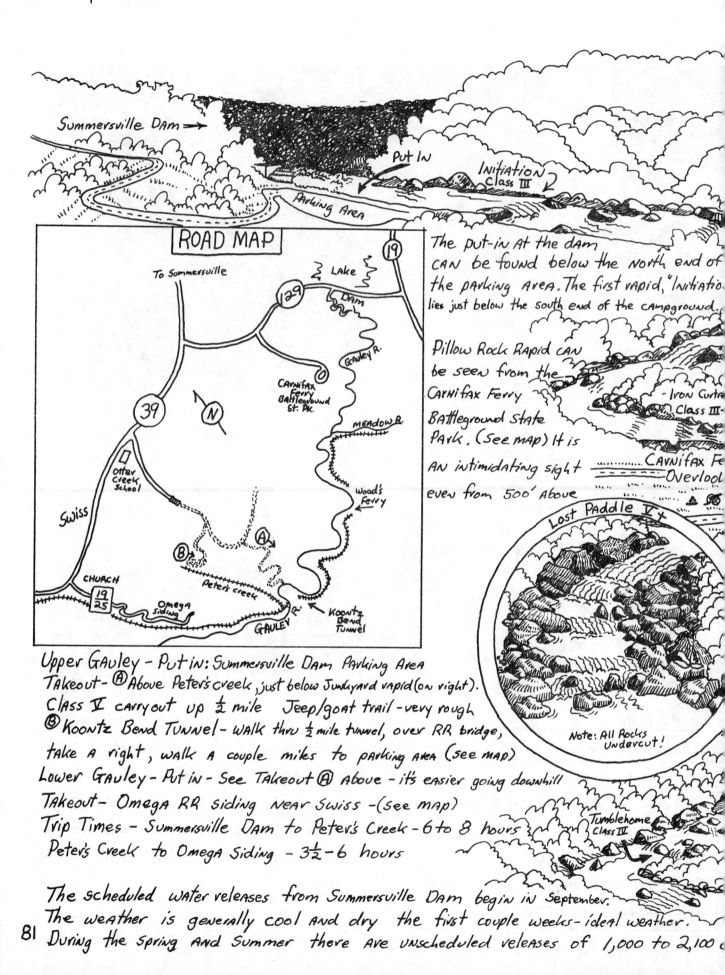

Summersville Dam →

Put In

Parking Area

Initiation Class III

ROAD MAP

To Summersville

19

Lake

129

Dam

Gauley R.

0

Carnifax Ferry Battleground St. Pk.

Meadow R.

39

N

Otter Creek School

Swiss

Wood's Ferry

Ⓐ

Ⓑ

CHURCH

19 25

Omega Siding

Peter's Creek

GAULEY R.

Koontz Bend Tunnel

GAULEY

The put-in at the dam can be found below the North end of the parking area. The first rapid, "Initiatio lies just below the south end of the campground.

Pillow Rock Rapid can be seen from the Carnifax Ferry Battleground State Park. (see map) It is an intimidating sight even from 500' above

- Iron Curta Class III

Carnifax Fe Overlool

Lost Paddle V +

Note: All Rocks Undercut!

Tumblehome Class IV

Upper Gauley - Put in: Summersville Dam Parking Area
Takeout- Ⓐ Above Peter's creek, just below Junkyard rapid (on right).
Class V carry out up ¼ mile   Jeep/goat trail -very rough
Ⓑ Koontz Tunnel - walk thru ½ mile tunnel, over RR bridge,
take a right, walk a couple miles to parking area (see map)
Lower Gauley - Put in - See Takeout Ⓐ Above - it's easier going downhill
Takeout- Omega RR siding near Swiss - (see map)
Trip Times - Summersville Dam to Peter's Creek - 6 to 8 hours
Peter's Creek to Omega Siding - 3½ - 6 hours

The scheduled water releases from Summersville Dam begin in September.
The weather is generally cool and dry the first couple weeks - ideal weather.
During the spring and summer there are unscheduled releases of 1,000 to 2,100 c

Near
Summersville, West Virginia

For water level, call Belva Gauge (304) 632-2071

Pillow Rock- Class V+ - This is the most difficult rapid on the river to run correctly (ie-upright) The only word for Pillow is awesome! it is 80 yds of insane H_2O terminated by a house-size rock on the left (the pillow) followed by another drop with a car-size chunk of sandstone splitting the current. To run the hero route, start left of center, thread your way back to the right to miss the Pillow Rock. To sneak, run far right of center (still class V). Scout this either way you plan to run. Carry on the right. Get enders from behind the rock at the bottom center.

Insignificant- Class V-
This is the first major rapid you hit (or hits you). Scout from the right bank. If you have any big trouble with it, the 2 mile upstream paddle should be considered.

mile 4

Pillow Rock- V+
HERO ROUTE
EDDY
SNEAK

MEADOW RIVER

mile 5

hip Rock Class III

Lost Paddle- Class V+ - Just below the confluence of the Meadow River (on the left) and the Gauley, Lost Paddle begins. This is the longest and 2nd most dangerous rapid on the Gauley. It is nearly half a mile long, steep, tricky, and full of undercut rocks (hence the name). Rescue is difficult because of the lack of big eddies and the speed of the current. Lost Paddle consists of several big drops preceeded by and followed by boat munching holes, terminating in a bizzare jumble of rocks. It is difficult to scout and/or portage. Bob Taylor, an expert K-1 paddler who was quite familiar with the Gauley, drowned near the bottom of Lost Paddle in 1977. This is no place to swim! If you can't roll 100%, the $\frac{1}{2}$ mile portage is a small price to pay for your good health.

Sweet's Falls - Class V

After Sweet's Falls paddlers can relax a bit. The river widens out and calms down for about 2½ miles until Wood's Ferry.

Sweet's Falls - Class V
This is one of those rare cases where the sneak route is harder than the hero route. For the sneak, run near the left bank, pick your way thru the numerous rocks and big drops.
Running the falls: Sweet's Falls is about half as bad as it looks. However - extreme caution must be exercized in choosing your route - Scout from right side. A good rule of thumb is to aim for the center of lowest point on the horizon line. Do not get close to the rock in the center - there's also a nasty roostertail-rock just left of your route. If you run too far to the right the water isn't very deep covering the rock with shallow aeriated water at the bottom - BOOM! If you run the correct route you'll also find the hole at the bottom is pretty mild-mannered; it may flip you but it won't hold you normally.

Recipe for Lost Paddle Rapid: Start with the 3 Keeneys (New R. Gorge), multiply by two, remove pools and eddies, sprinkle generously with undercut rocks, Add 3' to 5' of fast water, tilt 15° - serves thousands of crazy paddlers.

The name "Gauley" comes from the Indian name for the river - Tokebelloke ; "Gol-lee, that's falling water !"

Canyon Doors - Class III - This is one of the most spectacular sights in Gauley Canyon. The river curves left under a 300' sandstone cliff. Run right of center - This is a relatively long but fun rapid. It looks intimidating but, not to worry, it's easy.

Koontz Flume - Class IV (V) - put on your nose-plugs for this rapid. Run right of center and prepare to brace your way through the huge hole bottom right. Good surfing, etc.

Junkyard - Class III - Stay left all the way down.

Alternate Put In.

Iron Ring - Class VI - This is a particularly dangerous rapid. As a result of blasting a channel for logs to float through, a jagged, terminal obstruction was created midstream! What happens here is that the river necks down just above the jagged rock. About ⅓ of the water keeps on going down the right side - The rest recirculates above the obstruction before flushing over, under, around, and through it. Below the obstruction there is yet another hole that makes Woodall shoals look comical. To add to the objective danger of Iron Ring, we also have a situation where normally sane, mild-mannered paddlers decide to do a tango with the grim reaper. Running this rapid involves dropping off the right side into a monster hole, threading the needle, still on the right, around the obstruction and then out. Simple...easy —as long as you don't make one tiny little mistake. If you choose to run Iron Ring, do it right (upright) and use all possible safety precautions!

IRON RING-Class VI

Bad Hole

Obstruction

CARRY

Hole

...der Waves - great ...lay spot just below ...ood's Ferry.

Wood's Ferry Rapid - Class III
For shorter trip on the upper section, you can take out on the left side on the bend and carry out along Ramsey Branch to Leander.

On your first trip down the Gauley, don't camp anywhere near Summersville Dam if you want to get any sleep. The outflow shakes the ground and everything else nearby, literally! This artificially induced water-quake is not conducive to sleep or anything else that is restful or relaxing. -Magic Fingers on a regional scale.

mile 13

Five Boat Hole (A.K.A. Backender) Class III (IV).
A crescent-shaped hole preceeded by 75 yds of drops and big waves - Run right of Center.

Takeout- Koontz Bend
Railroad Tunnel to Peter's Creek - Watch for the tunnel opening on your left. The railbed appears to go straight into the mountain (which is exactly what it does). Stash boats in the bushes or high grass and proceed into the tunnel. It's as cold as... (use your imagination) and ½ mile long. If a train catches you inside, simply crouch down on either side of the railbed - (I hope that works- I've never been caught by a train in there). Cross the trestle & take the right-forking RR tracks to the parking area.

...tz Bend ...Tunnel

84

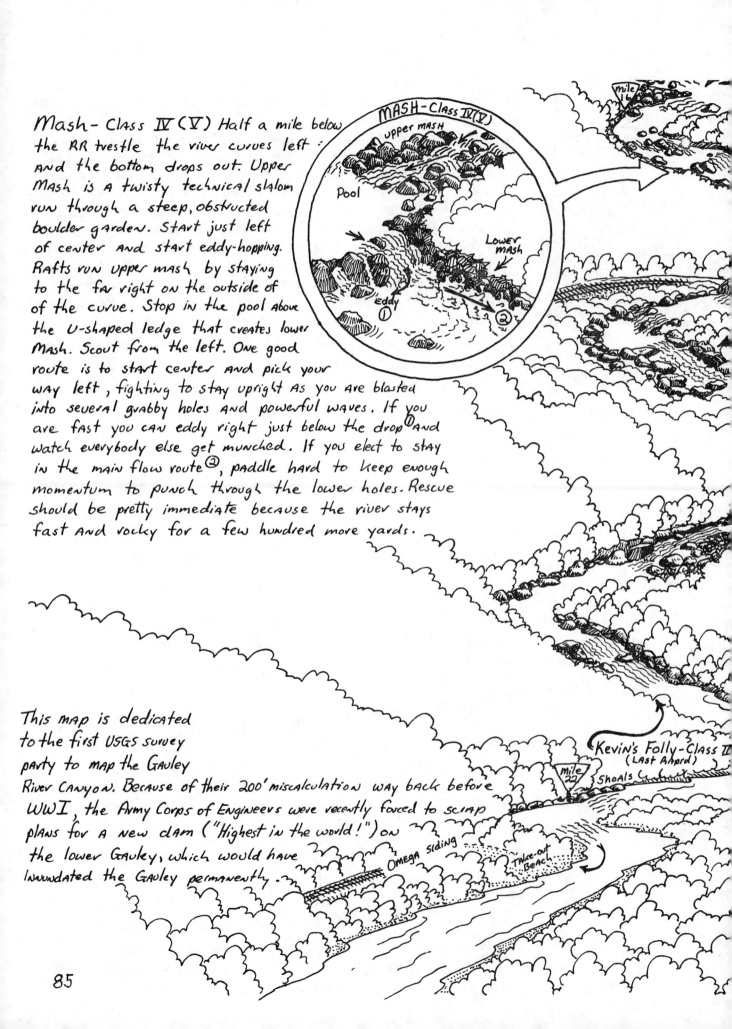

Mash - Class IV (V) Half a mile below
the RR trestle the river curves left
and the bottom drops out. Upper
Mash is a twisty technical slalom
run through a steep, obstructed
boulder garden. Start just left
of center and start eddy-hopping.
Rafts run upper mash by staying
to the far right on the outside of
of the curve. Stop in the pool above
the U-shaped ledge that creates lower
Mash. Scout from the left. One good
route is to start center and pick your
way left, fighting to stay upright as you are blasted
into several grabby holes and powerful waves. If you
are fast you can eddy right just below the drop ① and
watch everybody else get munched. If you elect to stay
in the main flow route ②, paddle hard to keep enough
momentum to punch through the lower holes. Rescue
should be pretty immediate because the river stays
fast and rocky for a few hundred more yards.

This map is dedicated
to the first USGS survey
party to map the Gauley
River Canyon. Because of their 200' miscalculation way back before
WW I, the Army Corps of Engineers were recently forced to scrap
plans for a new dam ("Highest in the world!") on
the lower Gauley, which would have
inundated the Gauley permanently.

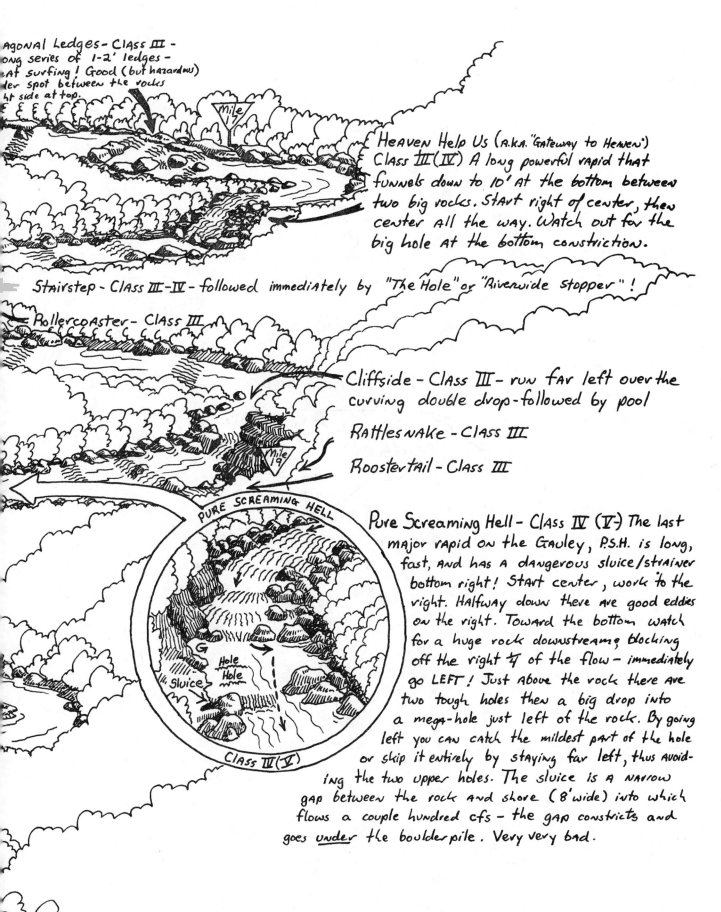

agonal Ledges - Class III -
ong series of 1-2' ledges -
at surfing! Good (but hazardous)
der spot between the rocks
ht side at top.

Heaven Help Us (a.k.a. "Gateway to Heaven")
Class III (IV) A long powerful rapid that
funnels down to 10' at the bottom between
two big rocks. Start right of center, then
center all the way. Watch out for the
big hole at the bottom constriction.

Stairstep - Class III-IV - followed immediately by "The Hole" or "Riverwide stopper"!

Rollercoaster - Class III

Cliffside - Class III - run far left over the
curving double drop - followed by pool

Rattlesnake - Class III

Roostertail - Class III

Pure Screaming Hell - Class IV (V-) The last
major rapid on the Gauley, P.S.H. is long,
fast, and has a dangerous sluice/strainer
bottom right! Start center, work to the
right. Halfway down there are good eddies
on the right. Toward the bottom watch
for a huge rock downstream, blocking
off the right ¼ of the flow - immediately
go LEFT! Just above the rock there are
two tough holes then a big drop into
a mega-hole just left of the rock. By going
left you can catch the mildest part of the hole
or skip it entirely by staying far left, thus avoiding the two upper holes. The sluice is a narrow
gap between the rock and shore (8' wide) into which
flows a couple hundred cfs - the gap constricts and
goes under the boulderpile. Very very bad.

PURE SCREAMING HELL

Sluice

Hole
Hole

Class IV (V)

Haw River

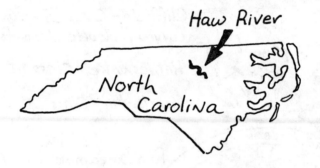

Haw River

North Carolina

HAW RIVER

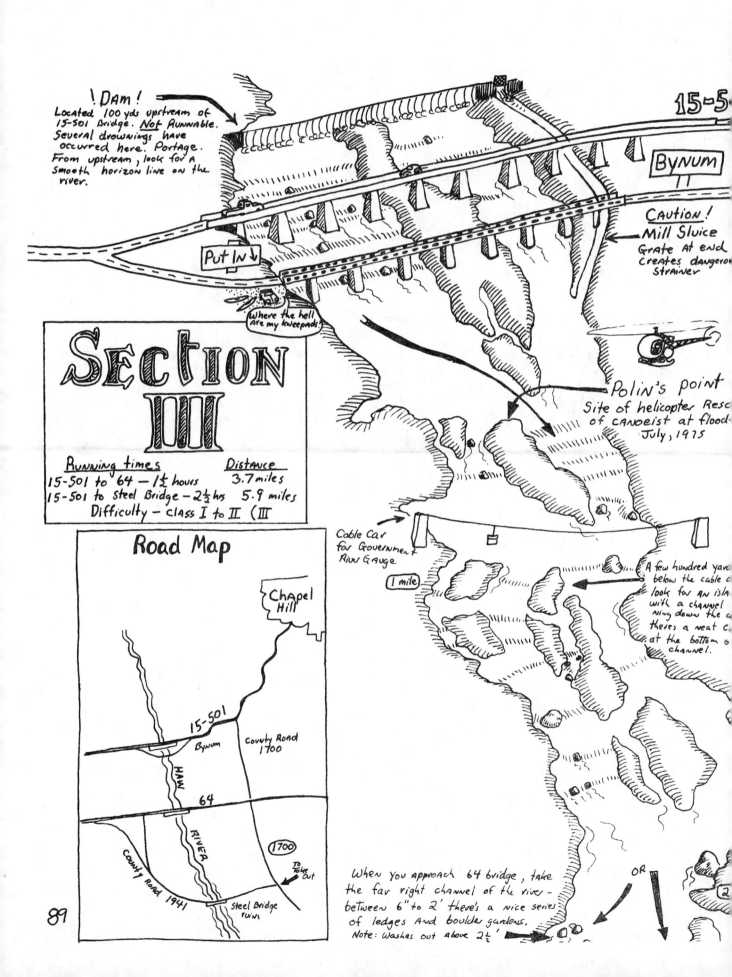

Haw River - Continued

!Dam!
Located 100 yds upstream of
15-501 Bridge. <u>Not Runnable</u>.
Several drownings have
occurred here. Portage.
From upstream, look for a
smooth horizon line on the
river.

Bynum

Put In ↓

Where the hell
Are my kneepads!

Caution!
Mill Sluice
Grate At end
Creates dangerou
Strainer

Polin's point
Site of helicopter Resc
of canoeist at flood
July, 1975

Section III

Running times   **Distance**
15-501 to 64 - 1½ hours   3.7 miles
15-501 to Steel Bridge - 2½ hrs   5.9 miles
Difficulty - class I to II (III

Cable Car
for Government
River Gauge

1 mile

A few hundred yar
below the cable c
look for an isla
with a channel
ning down the c
there's a neat c
at the bottom o
channel.

Road Map

Chapel
Hill

15-501

Bynum   County Road
1700

HAW

64

RIVER

1700

County Road 1941

To
Take
Out

Steel Bridge
ruins

89

OR

2

When you approach 64 bridge, take
the far right channel of the river -
between 6" to 2' there's a nice series
of ledges and boulder gardens.
Note: Washes out Above 2½'

Highway 64
4 miles

Chapel Hill - 11 miles

Warning!
!!! Dangerous ⬇ River !!!

Several incidents involving various combinations of high water, inexperience, and abject stupidity, have resulted in several drownings, numerous helicopter evacuations, etc. Do everyone a favor - <u>be aware</u> - Know how to recognize a floodstage river and stay the hell off it. If you do get in trouble, at least <u>try</u> to affect your own rescue. It would look better for all paddlers if the public (and interested officials) could see that we can take care of ourselves.

River Safety

Never Boat Alone
Know how to swim
Know your Ability - don't overestimate it!
Wear your P.F.D.
Wear proper clothing - wetsuits are mandatory in cold weather
Know the river.
Respect the river.
Beware of Dam controlled rivers !!!
It is the innocent-looking low dam that is the <u>most</u> dangerous to the paddler.

American Red Cross

S.R. 1700

Great Blue Heron

N

Pork Barrel Politics as "Bad Art" - Conceived nearly 25 years ago as a good way to create 250 plus miles of expensive lakeshore property in an "economically depressed" county, the B.*Everett Jordan Lake's future is still up in the air. Suffering from construction defects, 200% cost overruns, and heavy opposition from a variety of interests, the project (already 11 years late) faces another two year delay. This will likely push the project cost well over 100 million dollars. According to the Corps of Engineer's own environmental assessment (published mid-70's) the lake will probably be an eutrophic green-pea soup, contaminated with heavy metals (mercury, et al) and colliform bacteria (usually found in raw sewage) - Not suitable for "contact recreation." You can't swim in it, ski on it, drink from it, and the fish are poisonous... enjoy the lake, ya'll. Also coming soon to Chatham County: Sharon Harris Nuclear Power Plant and (wonder of wonders) a proposed Nuclear and hazardous chemical waste dump. And <u>SO</u> convenient to the Triangle Area, too!
   *"B" for boondoggle

Raleigh
24 miles

Haw River - Continued

Wildlife - deer, muskrat, beaver, raccoons
wild turkeys (not the human variety)
great blue heron, turkey vulture,
red-tailed hawk, etc.
Note: Bigfoot has not been sighted in
this area.

River Gauges - unofficial piling gauges are painted in
orange at the west end of old Bynum bridge and at Hwy. 64
bridge. The USGS gauge is downstream of Bynum. The
conversion of USGS reading to piling gauge reading is
USGS reading minus 5'.

3 miles

River Gauge on
2nd Piling

Pittsboro
4 miles

PUT IN

PATH

To Steel Bridge Ruins

Lunch Stop
Rapid
Class II-III

Class III-
Rapid

Gabriel's Bend - Class III (III+) - This long Class III
rapid has inspired many gothic river tales, usually told
by boaters who flipped at the top and swam it.
The easiest route is to run just left of
center all the way through (avoiding rocks &
holes as they appear). The **BEST** way to run
it is by eddy-hopping the whole thing. Above
2½', watch for big beautiful waves between Ⓐ
→ Ⓑ. At Ⓑ, just right of center, is a real
boat-eating hole at high water. The bottom
ledge Ⓒ is a great surfing hole between
1½'-3½'. At lower water, watch your head if
you flip because it's very shallow there.
It's easy to eddy-hop from the bottom back
up to the top drop Ⓐ - good boaters get to
run it twice. Rescue swimmers fast because
Moose Jaw Falls is just below! Warning: on sunny days
in Spring and Summer, Gabriel's Bend is a ZOO!

Gabriel's Bend
Class III

BLUFF

Put In

Gauge (painted on 1st pylon)
6" below 0" - minimum level
0" to 1' - optimum level
1' to 2' - Advanced paddlers
2' to 3' - Expert Water
Above 3' - Extremely Dangerous!

Section IV

Running time
1 hour

Distance
2.2 miles

Difficulty - Class I, II, and III

S.R. 1700 to steel bridge (see road map)

If you eat it...

float on your back
stay upstream of swamped boat
keep feet pointed downstream
relax & watch for calm water

Ocean Boulevard Big Waves Above 1'

4 miles

The ubiquitous plastic milk jug
Used in making certain plastic kayaks (Also makes a good bailer)

milk

cut

CURRENT

Harold's Tombstone
Class III-

Aiieee!

Bonk!

Watch out for Strainers, snags and overhanging branches

The Slot

Moosejaw Falls
Class II-III

92

Haw River — Continued

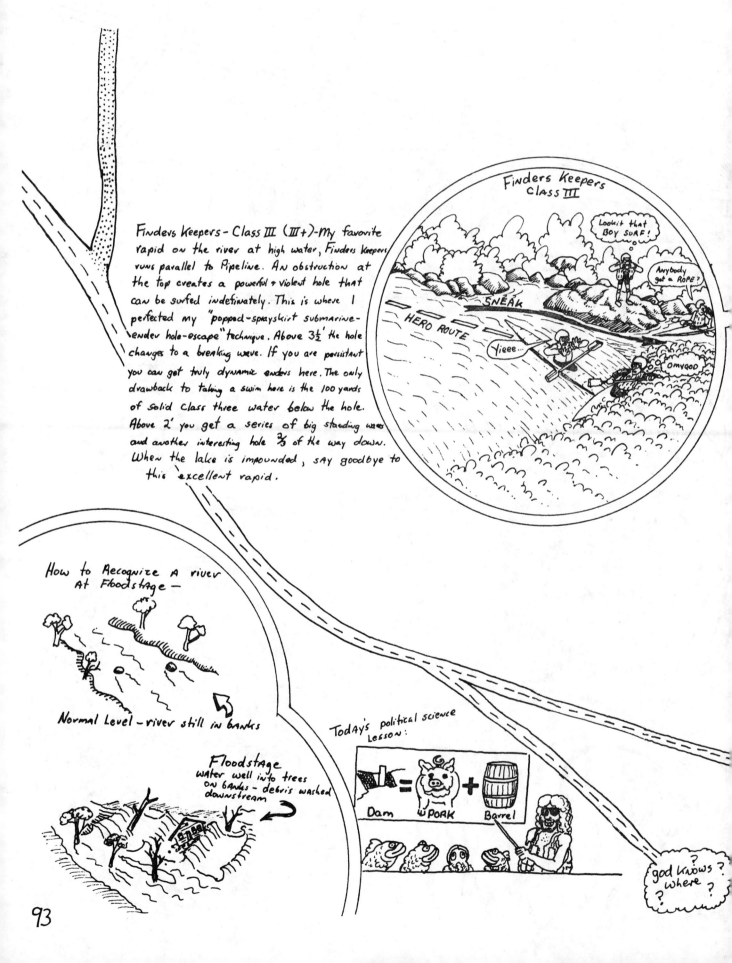

Finders Keepers – Class III (III+) – My favorite rapid on the river at high water, Finders Keepers runs parallel to Pipeline. An obstruction at the top creates a powerful & violent hole that can be surfed indefinately. This is where I perfected my "popped-sprayskirt submarine-ender hole-escape" technique. Above 3½' the hole changes to a breaking wave. If you are persistant you can get truly dynamic enders here. The only drawback to taking a swim here is the 100 yards of solid class three water below the hole. Above 2' you get a series of big standing waves and another interesting hole ⅔ of the way down. When the lake is impounded, say goodbye to this excellent rapid.

Finders Keepers
Class III

Lookit that BOY SURF!

Anybody got a ROPE?

SNEAK

HERO ROUTE

Yieee...

OMYGOD

How to Recognize A river At Floodstage —

Normal Level – river still in banks

Floodstage water well into trees on banks – debris washed downstream

Today's political science lesson:

Dam = W PORK + Barrel

god knows? where?

93

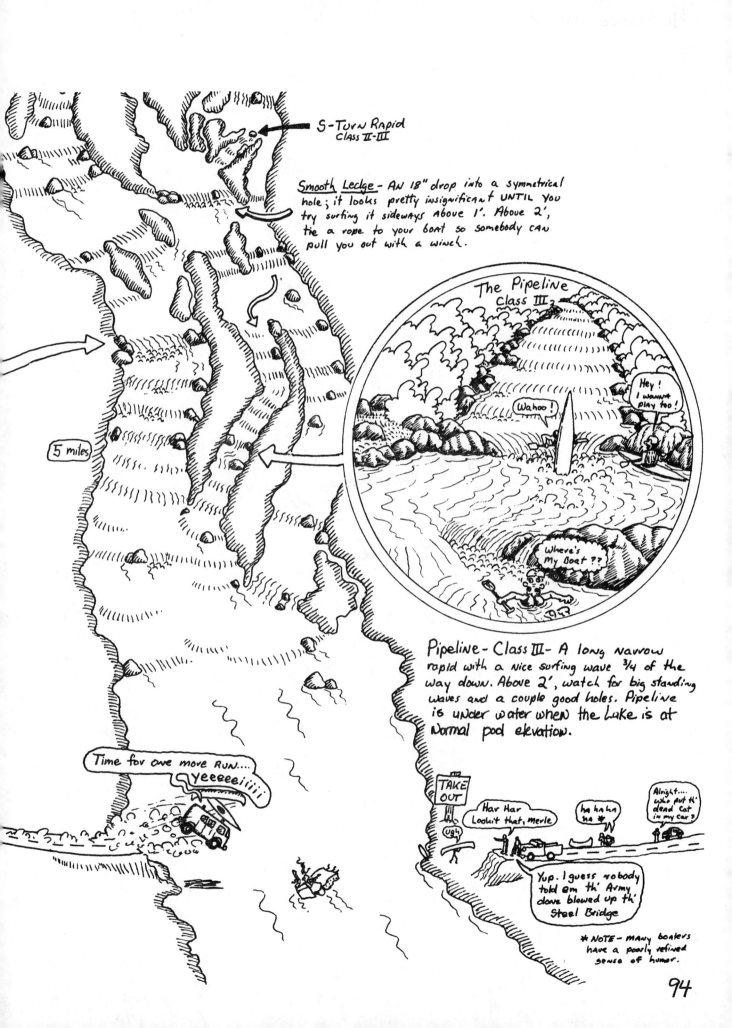

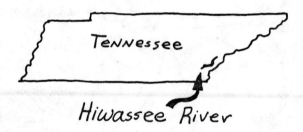

Tennessee

Hiwassee River

Hiwassee River

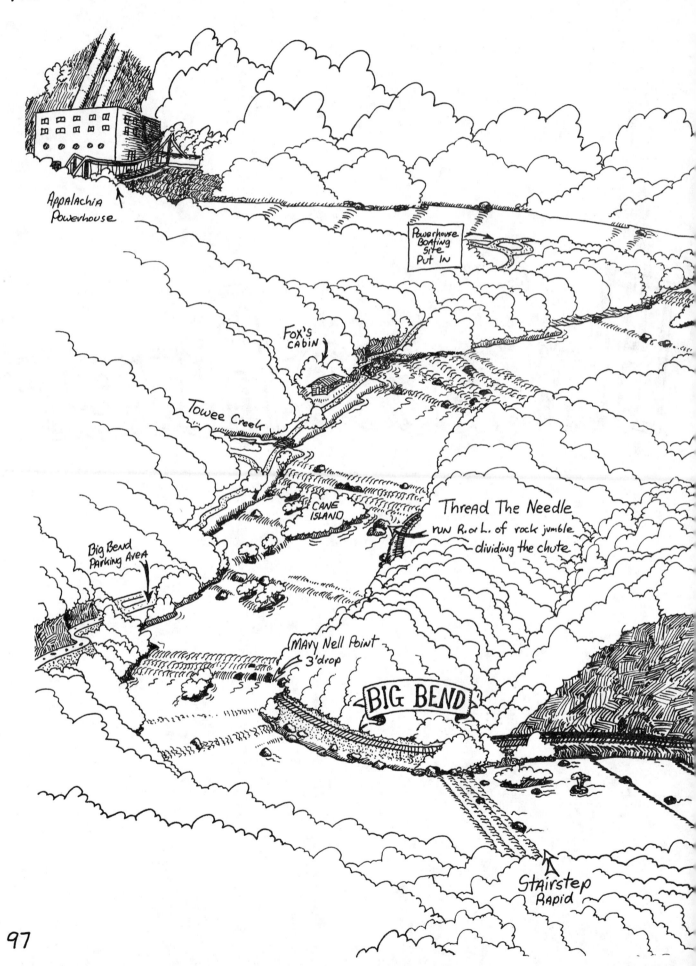

Appalachia Powerhouse

Powerhouse Boating Site Put In

Fox's Cabin

Towee Creek

CANE ISLAND

Thread The Needle
run R. or L. of rock jumble
dividing the chute

Big Bend Parking Area

MAvy Nell Point
3' drop

BIG BEND

Stairstep Rapid

A Tennessee State Scenic River
Near Reliance, Tn.

The Hiwassee River is an exceptionally beautiful river. Water flow is controlled by T.V.A. but frequent discharges make the river runnable even in mid and late summer. This is an excellent river for family outings, canoeing, tubing, rafting and beginning whitewater instruction. Note: As a rule, the best whitewater will be encountered by staying near the left shore and running left of most islands.

General Information

Overall Difficulty : Class II (AWA)
Gradient: 15 feet per mile
Scenery : excellent
Water Quality : good to excellent
Water Temp.: damned cold !
Length of Trip: Powerhouse to Reliance
— 5.5 miles

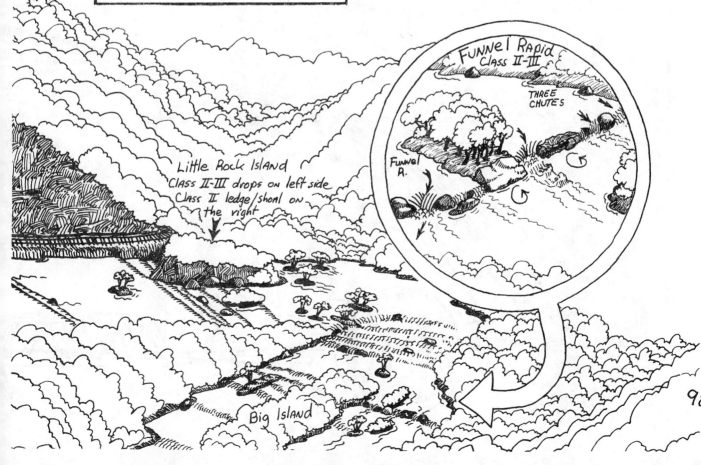

Little Rock Island
Class II-III drops on left side
Class II ledge/shoal on the right

Funnel Rapid
Class II-III

THREE CHUTES

Funnel R.

Big Island

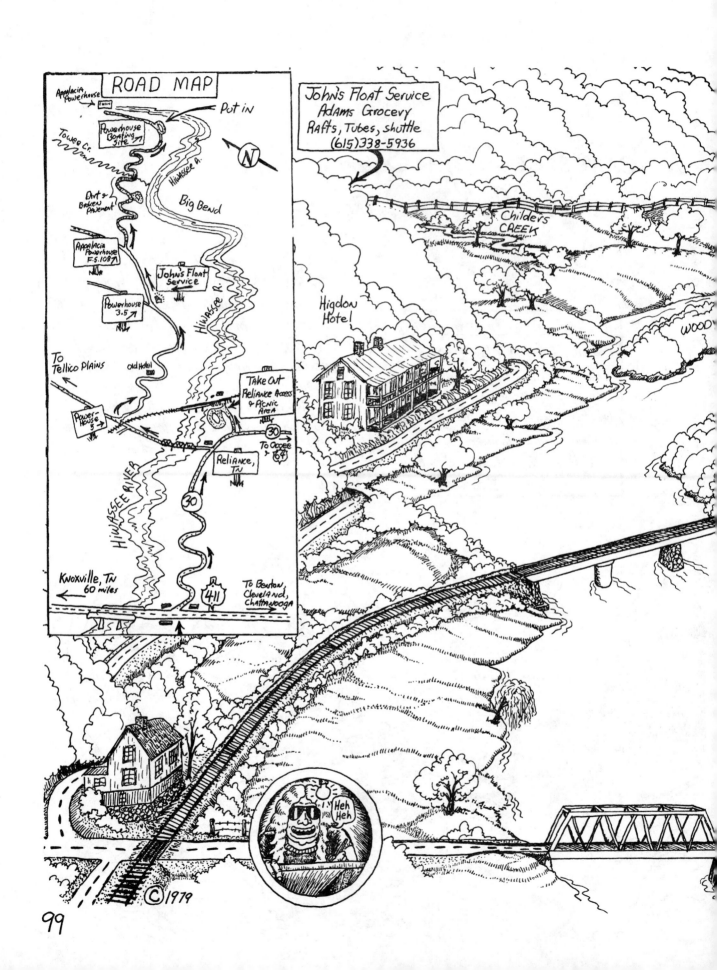

ROAD MAP

Appalacia Powerhouse

Put in

Powerhouse Boating Site

Towee Cr.

Hiwassee R.

Big Bend

Dirt & Broken Pavement

Appalacia Powerhouse F.S.108↑

John's Float Service

Powerhouse 3.5↑

To Tellico Plains

Old Hotel

Hiwassee R.

Take Out Reliance Access & Picnic Area

Power house 5↑

30

To Ocoee 64

Reliance, TN

30

Hiwassee River

Knoxville, TN 60 miles

411

To Benton, Cleveland, Chattanooga

John's Float Service
Adams Grocery
Rafts, Tubes, shuttle
(615)338-5936

Childers CREEK

Higdon Hotel

WOOD

Heh Heh

©1979

Big Island

Big Lost Creek

Devil's Shoals
Class II-III
(III)

This map is dedicated to my lovely friend, Barrie Wallace, who, against all odds, graduated high school and stayed sane.

ISLAND

Hot Showers

CAMPGROUND

Hiwassee Outfitters
Raft Trips

FOOD

COLD DRINKS

Hiwassee Outfitters
(615) 338-8142
Special Thanks to Denis Berney for his help and hospitality!

Reliance Access & Picnic Area
Take Out

Pioneer Church
And School House

Webb's Float Service, Inc.
Raft & tube rentals, Post office
food, souvenirs, Shuttle service
"Home of Bacchus"
(615) 338-2373

TEXACO
Post Office   RAFTS

WEBB BRO TEXACO

RELIANCE

U.S.
30

Built - 1912

Webb's landing –
private – No parking,
etc.

100

Alabama

Locust Fork
of the
Warrior River

LOCUST FORK

Locust Fork - Continued

The Locust Fork of the Warrior has for years been the most popular whitewater run in North-central Alabama. The Hwy 231/79 Bridge to Nectar covered bridge section, with its 24 f.p.m. gradient, is a great Class III (III-IV$_{IV}$) run, with some beautiful scenery along the way. Water quality is poor because of discharges from the Blountsville chicken plant and runoff from the heavily stripmined hills upstream. The Fork is runnable usually all Spring and after rainstorms throughout the year. The run is highly recommended if you are in the area.

The U.S.G.S. gauge is located just upstream of the Hwy. 79 bridge, on the south bank. The minimum level is 2.0' (very low) with levels of 2.8' to 3.3' being ideal. The river is most difficult at levels between 4' and 6' — things are big and pushy but not too washed out. This level is for advanced-intermediate to expert paddlers. Above 6' the river turns into a big wave/hole extravaganza and most rapids get totally washed out. The main hazard at floodstage is the banks of the river; the river gets so far out of its banks that a swimmer must thread thru a deadly obstacle course of trees in incredibly fast water to reach the shore. Every Spring the same tragedy seems to repeat itself — floodstage + Army surplus raft + beer + no life-jacket and somebody gets wrapped around a tree and drowns. The river has been successfully run at 9' in open boats, but not without some near misses.

Now for the bad news - Locals and paddlers have never really gotten along here. Every now and then the natives get restless and the local constabulary tows some unfortunate paddler's car away. There is no reliable pattern to this behavior, so you're on your own. In general, obey "No Parking" and "No Tresspassing" signs and never ever get caught with beer (dry county) or controlled substances!

Historical Note - Local vs. Paddler relations got real hot (excuse the pun) in the Spring of 1977. The river was being considered for Wild & Scenic River classification, a canoe shop opened up on the river, and the local high school football star drowned on the river at floodstage. The locals got fed up with this whitewater business altogether. All of a sudden, trees got cut down across some rapids, barbed wire got strung across the river, and paddlers' cars got towed to a garage 40 miles away. Then the KKK posters appeared on trees, utility poles, and on the canoe shop sign. The word around Blount County was that something was going to happen real soon.

On the night of May 26, the canoe shop owners were at the Cleveland mayor's house trying to get things cooled down a little. They talked while the mayor swatted flies and contributed an occasional "uh huh" to the conversation. After a while a volunteer fireman burst in yelling "Fire! Fire!". "Where? Where?" the owners hollered back. "YOUR place", the fireman replied. Sure enough, it was.

The local police chief, his son, and a landowner were indicted for arson on the basis of an investigation by the State Attorney General's office. They were found "not guilty" by a Blount County jury in 1978.

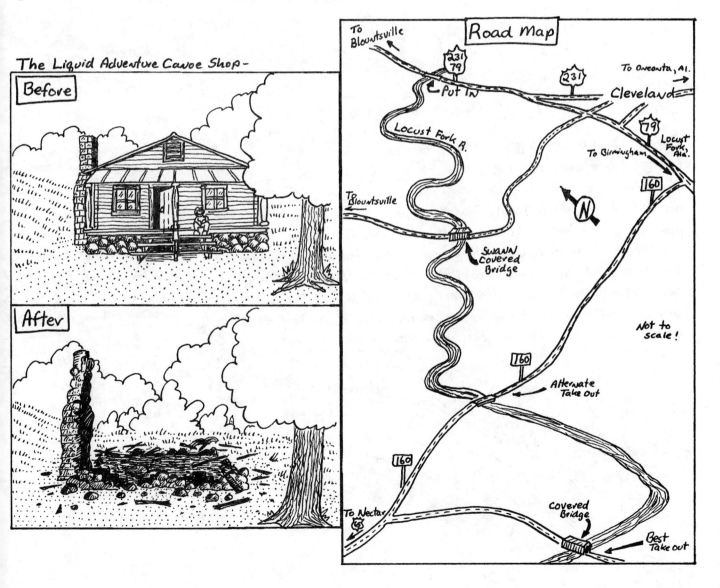

The Liquid Adventure Canoe Shop –

Before

After

Road Map

104

Locust Fork - Continued

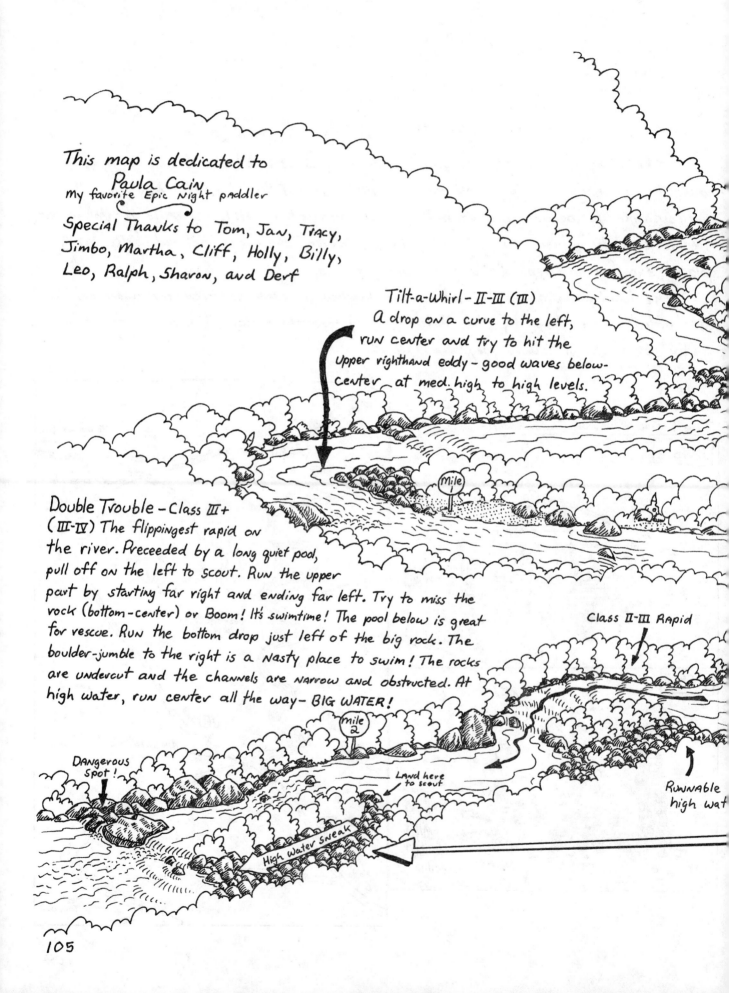

This map is dedicated to
Paula Cain
my favorite Epic Night paddler

Special Thanks to Tom, Jan, Tracy,
Jimbo, Martha, Cliff, Holly, Billy,
Leo, Ralph, Sharon, and Derf

Tilt-a-Whirl - II-III (III)
A drop on a curve to the left,
run center and try to hit the
upper righthand eddy - good waves below-
center at med. high to high levels.

Mile 1

Double Trouble - Class III+
(III-IV) The flippingest rapid on
the river. Preceeded by a long quiet pool,
pull off on the left to scout. Run the upper
part by starting far right and ending far left. Try to miss the
rock (bottom-center) or Boom! It's swimtime! The pool below is great
for rescue. Run the bottom drop just left of the big rock. The
boulder-jumble to the right is a nasty place to swim! The rocks
are undercut and the channels are narrow and obstructed. At
high water, run center all the way- BIG WATER!

Class II-III Rapid

mile 2

Dangerous
Spot!

Land here
to scout

Runnable
high wat

High Water Sneak

105

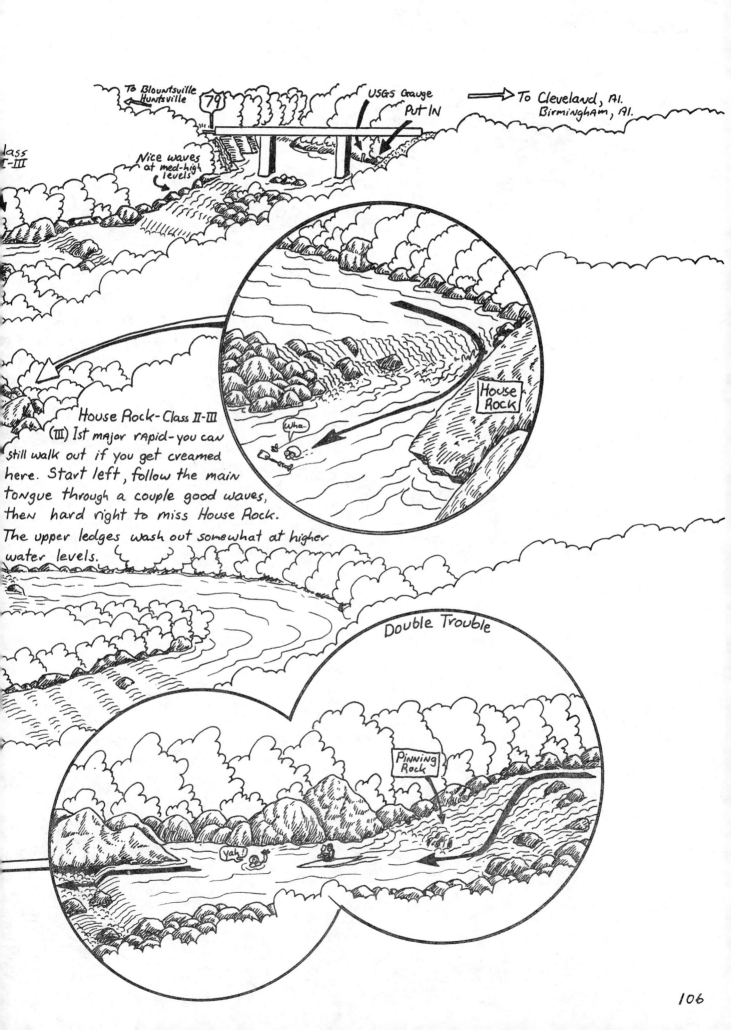

To Blountsville
Huntsville

79

USGS Gauge
Put IN

To Cleveland, Al.
Birmingham, Al.

Class
II-III

Nice waves at med-high levels

House Rock

Wha..

House Rock- Class II-III
(III) Ist major rapid-you can
still walk out if you get creamed
here. Start left, follow the main
tongue through a couple good waves,
then hard right to miss House Rock.
The upper ledges wash out somewhat at higher
water levels.

Double Trouble

Pinning Rock

yah!

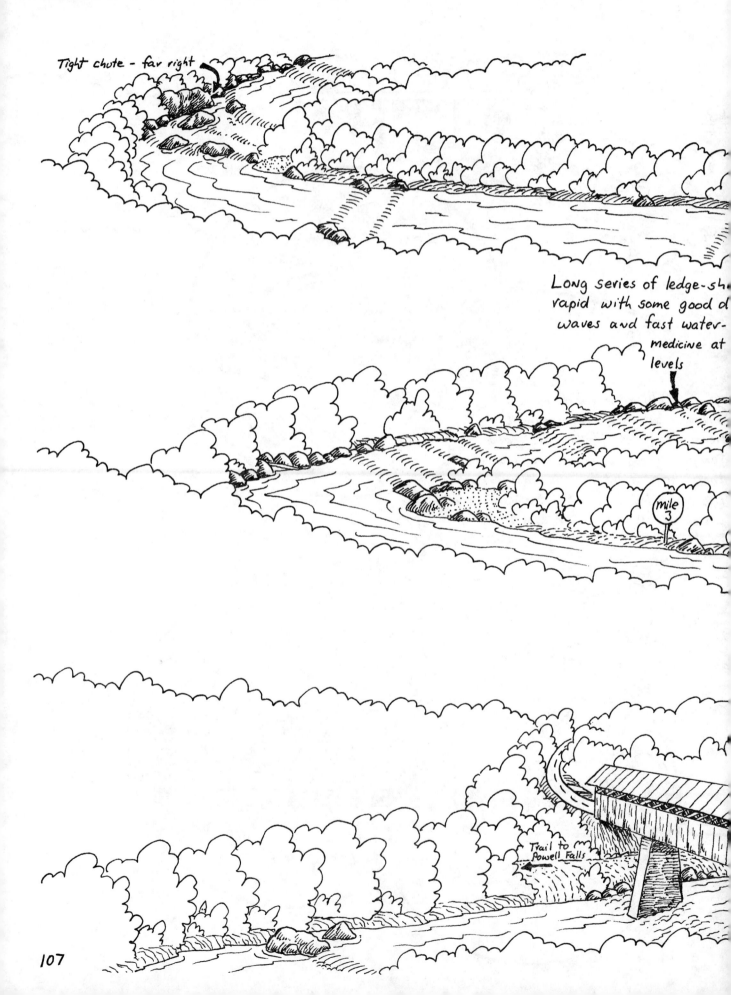

Tight chute - far right

Long series of ledge-sh.
rapid with some good d.
waves and fast water-
medicine at
levels

mile
3

Trail to
Powell Falls

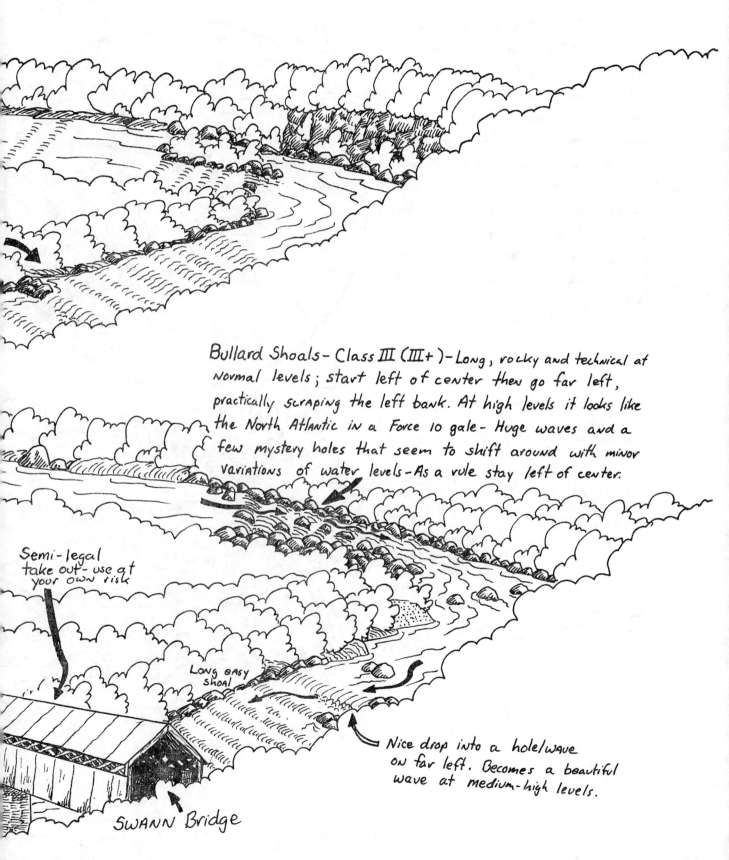

Bullard Shoals – Class III (III+) – Long, rocky and technical at normal levels; start left of center then go far left, practically scraping the left bank. At high levels it looks like the North Atlantic in a Force 10 gale – Huge waves and a few mystery holes that seem to shift around with minor variations of water levels – As a rule stay left of center.

Semi-legal take out – use at your own risk

LONG EASY SHOAL

Nice drop into a hole/wave on far left. Becomes a beautiful wave at medium-high levels.

SWANN Bridge

Locust Fork – Continued

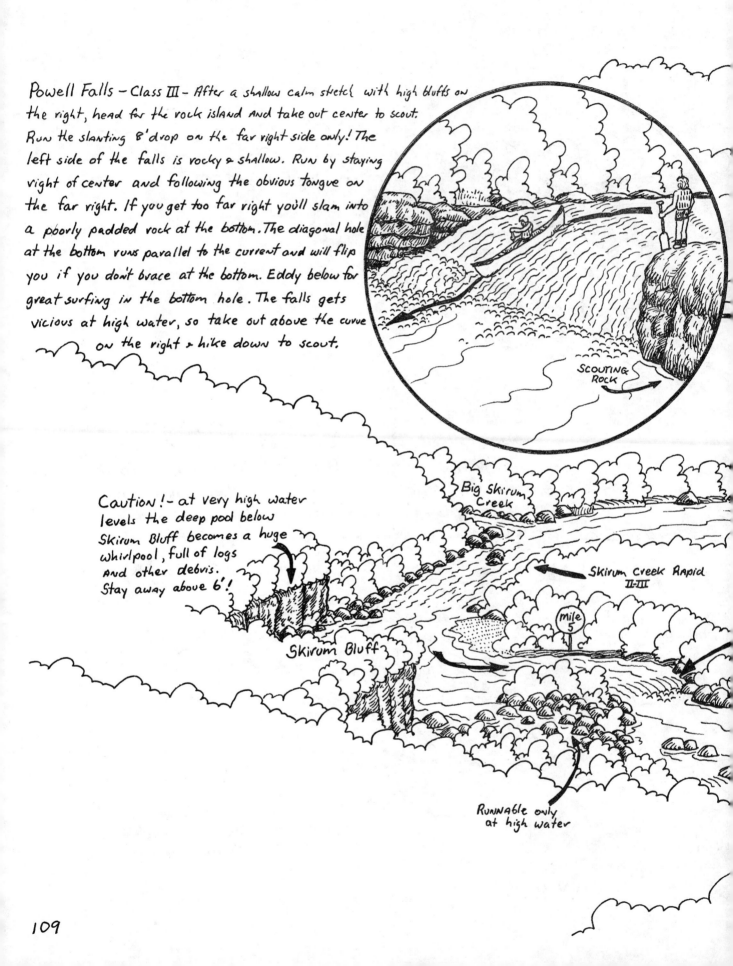

Powell Falls – Class III – After a shallow calm stretch with high bluffs on the right, head for the rock island and take out center to scout. Run the slanting 8' drop on the far right side only! The left side of the falls is rocky & shallow. Run by staying right of center and following the obvious tongue on the far right. If you get too far right you'll slam into a poorly padded rock at the bottom. The diagonal hole at the bottom runs parallel to the current and will flip you if you don't brace at the bottom. Eddy below for great surfing in the bottom hole. The falls gets vicious at high water, so take out above the curve on the right & hike down to scout.

SCOUTING ROCK

Caution! – at very high water levels the deep pool below Skirum Bluff becomes a huge whirlpool, full of logs and other debris. Stay away above 6'!

Skirum Bluff

Big Skirum Creek

Skirum Creek Rapid II-III

mile 5

Runnable only at high water

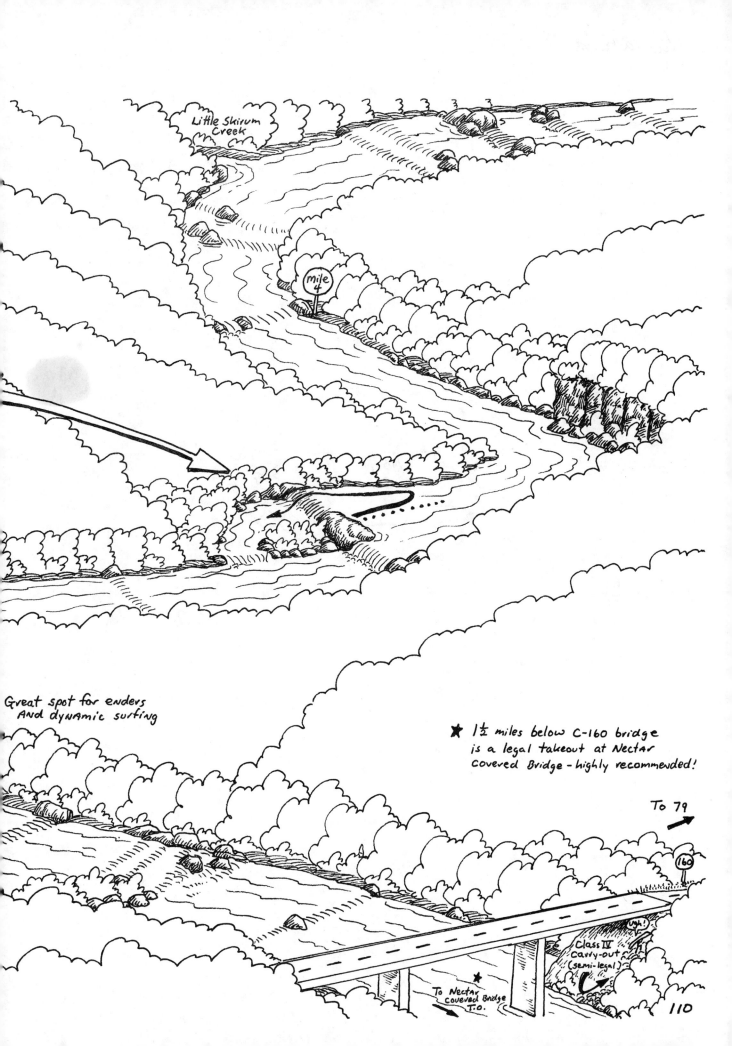

Little Skirum Creek

mile 4

Great spot for enders
And dynamic surfing

★ 1½ miles below C-160 bridge
is a legal takeout at Nectar
Covered Bridge - highly recommended!

To 79

160

Ugh!

Class IV
Carry-out
(semi-legal)

To Nectar
Covered Bridge
T.O.

110

Nantahala River

North
Carolina

Nantahala
River

NANTAHALA

Powerhouse

Old Put In

NEW PUT-IN

Restrooms

19

Andrews
Chattanooga
Atlanta

Long
Class II-III
Rapid

Patton's Run
Class III+

OOF!

EEK

Har Har!

Isle of
Dumping

Thud!

Tumble Dry

Pop'n Run

mile 1

Winding
Stairs
Road

mile 2

Gauging
Station

Pyramid Rock

Brrr...

Patton's Run — Class III + — 100 yards below the new put-in the river curves hard right, drops and slams into a large boulder on the left. Run this by staying far right (just off the right bank) and staying on the inside of the curve. Brace thru the bottom waves and eddy right or left to bail. Rescue swimmers quickly before they get into the II-III stuff below. This rapid is named for Charlie Patton (deceased), one of the grand old men of Nantahala open boaters.

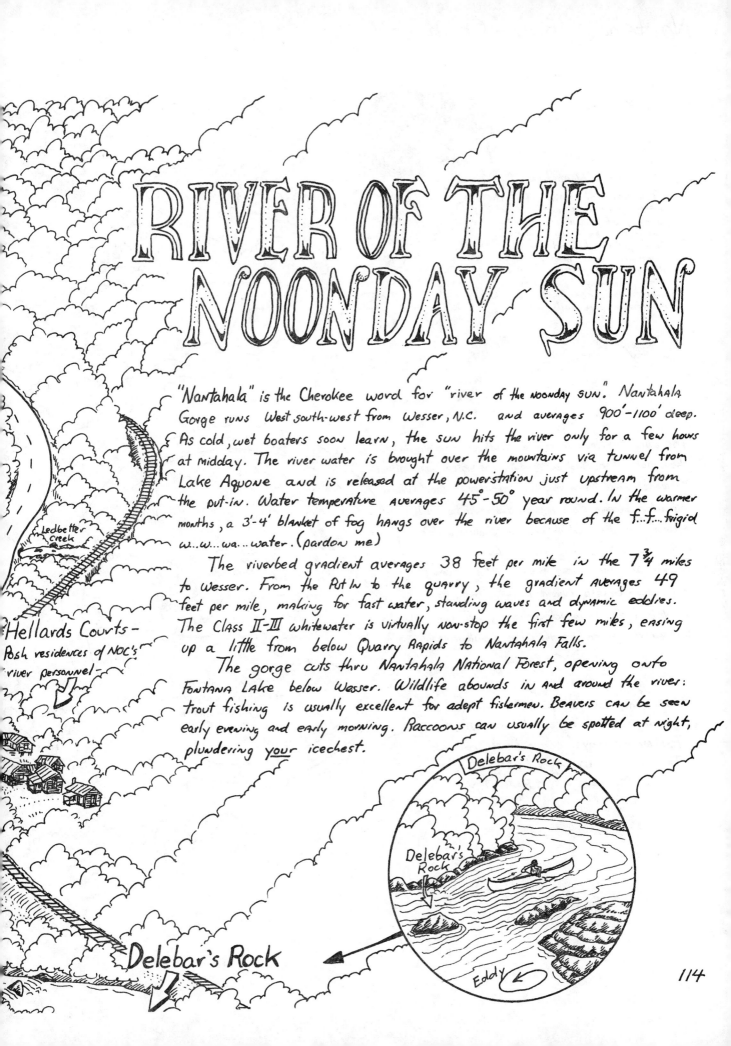

RIVER OF THE NOONDAY SUN

"Nantahala" is the Cherokee word for "river of the noonday sun". Nantahala Gorge runs West south-west from Wesser, N.C. and averages 900'-1100' deep. As cold, wet boaters soon learn, the sun hits the river only for a few hours at midday. The river water is brought over the mountains via tunnel from Lake Aquone and is released at the powerstation just upstream from the put-in. Water temperature averages 45°-50° year round. In the warmer months, a 3'-4' blanket of fog hangs over the river because of the f...f...frigid w...w...wa...water. (pardon me)

The riverbed gradient averages 38 feet per mile in the 7¾ miles to Wesser. From the Put In to the quarry, the gradient averages 49 feet per mile, making for fast water, standing waves and dynamic eddies. The Class II-III whitewater is virtually non-stop the first few miles, easing up a little from below Quarry Rapids to Nantahala Falls.

The gorge cuts thru Nantahala National Forest, opening onto Fontana Lake below Wesser. Wildlife abounds in and around the river: trout fishing is usually excellent for adept fishermen. Beavers can be seen early evening and early morning. Raccoons can usually be spotted at night, plundering your icechest.

Ledbetter Creek

Hellards Courts — Posh residences of NOC's river personnel —

Delebar's Rock

Delebar's Rock

Delebar's Rock

Eddy

Nantahala River - Continued

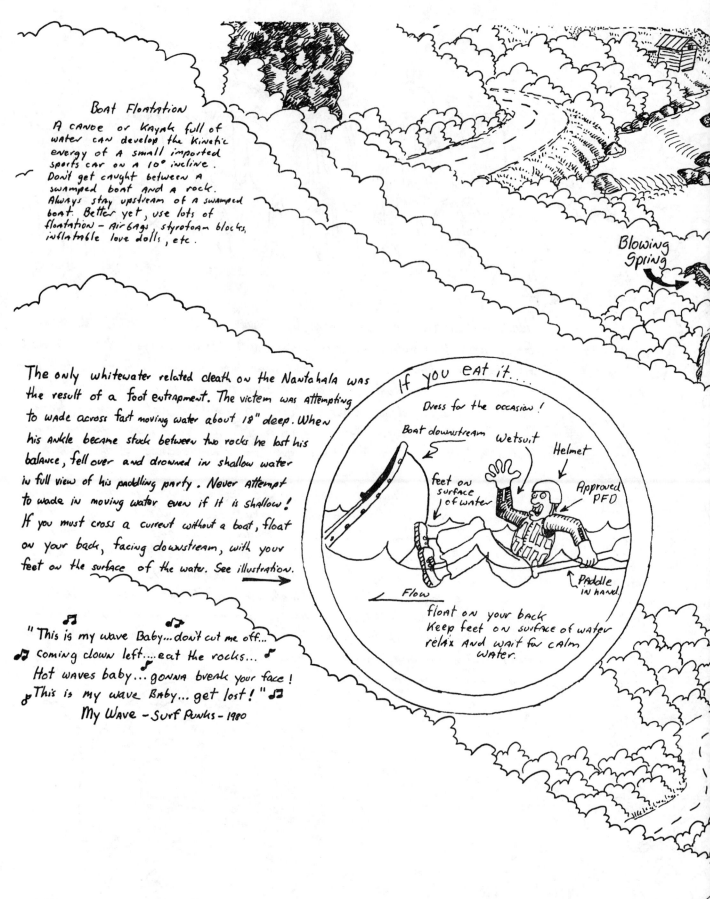

Boat Floatation

A canoe or kayak full of water can develop the kinetic energy of a small imported sports car on a 10° incline. Don't get caught between a swamped boat and a rock. Always stay upstream of a swamped boat. Better yet, use lots of floatation - air bags, styrofoam blocks, inflatable love dolls, etc.

The only whitewater related death on the Nantahala was the result of a foot entrapment. The victim was attempting to wade across fast moving water about 18" deep. When his ankle became stuck between two rocks he lost his balance, fell over and drowned in shallow water in full view of his paddling party. Never attempt to wade in moving water even if it is shallow! If you must cross a current without a boat, float on your back, facing downstream, with your feet on the surface of the water. See illustration. →

"This is my wave Baby...don't cut me off...
coming down left....eat the rocks...
Hot waves baby...gonna break your face!
This is my wave Baby... get lost!"
   My Wave - Surf Punks - 1980

If you eat it....

Dress for the occasion!

Boat downstream   Wetsuit   Helmet

feet on surface of water   Approved PFO

Flow   Paddle in hand.

float on your back
keep feet on surface of water
relax and wait for calm water.

Blowing Spring

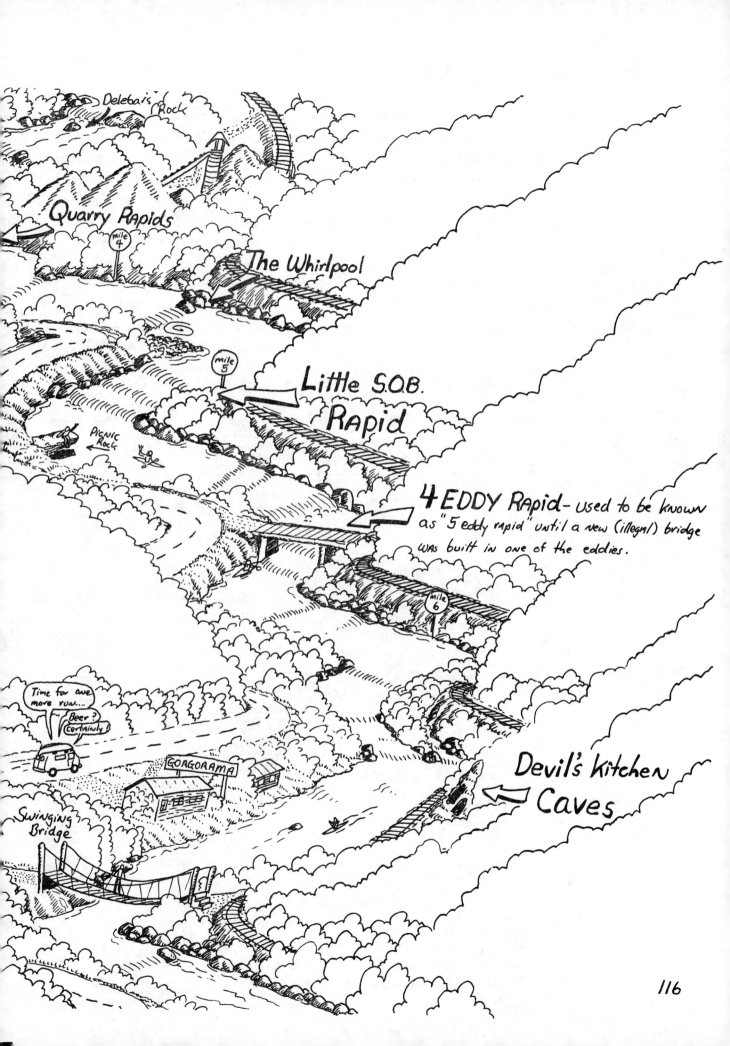

116

Nantahala River - continued

Nantahala Falls - Class III (III-IV)

This has to be the best know rapid on earth. In the 60's it was rated Class V (Randy Carter). In the early 70's, Bob Benner rated it IV to V. As equipment and technique have improved over the last few years, the rating has dropped to Class III (III-IV high water). The falls didn't get any easier; we just got better. Run the falls by starting far river left Ⓐ and cutting diagonally right after the first drop Ⓑ, ending center and bracing through the violent wave at the bottom Ⓒ. Eddy right or left to bail. Swimmers and decked boaters beware — Just below the falls there are several submerged rocks which can bust boats, heads, and knees. Avoid the upper hole Ⓓ in the center of the top drop. The hydraulic will hold boats and bodies for minutes. If you get stuck in it, try to get to the main jet on the left. Usually if you relax, the hole will spit you out after a few recirculations.

THE FORT

CHANGING Rooms

Laundry Stuff

Motel

Nantahala Outdoor Center

Store: outdoor equipment, boats, food

Restaurant

OLD TAKE O

Wha..

GAS

NANTAHALA OUTDOOR COURSE

LOST mine CAMPGROUND

Public restrooms & changing rooms

Special thanks to "Honest" John Barber for his assistance in revising this map.

Public Parking Take Out Restrooms, Changing rooms Raft Rentals

Food !

BONK

DAMN!

R

Did you tie the boats on good?

yeah.. sure

To: Asheville Bryson City Cullowee

19

great god a'mighty!

To Weisser Falls overlook

Kayakers are just failed Hell's Angels in boats

This map is dedicated to Holly Wallace (a.k.a. "Dragon Lady") who listened to my river stories for 3 years before she got sick of them.

New River Gorge

West Virginia

New River

NEW RIVER GORGE

New River Gorge - Continued

The New is an old old river. Exactly how old it really is seems to be a matter of dispute. Some sources say it's the oldest river in North America, predating the tectonic plate collision (kind of a geological fender-bender) that formed the Appalachian Mountains. A geologist friend of mine says those estimates are greatly exaggerated. Suffice it to say that the New isn't going to hobble away anytime soon, which is lucky for us. Known as the "Grand Canyon of the East", the New Gorge is an incredible run for paddlers who are used to small, steep, low-volume rivers. Above 2.0' on the Fayette Station gauge it gets huge and keeps on getting bigger until it washes out at some ungodly level (19 feet!?). I have heard some fairly sane outfitters and boaters talk seriously about actual 20' waves at very high levels. "The nice thing about it," they say, "is the waves are 90-100' apart, so you've got lots of time to recover from the preceeding wave."—which sounds so crazy it's probably true. There are some honest-to-god six and seven foot waves at a level of 3', but there my experience runs out.

The surprisingly mild gradient (12-15 feet per mile) combines with the high volume and constricted riverbed (below mile 8) to create some classic whitewater in the gorge. Most of the rapids are fairly straightforeward and not too difficult at medium levels (2.0'-3.0'). The major rapids are not so much true Class V's as they are five-esque. As long as you've got a good roll and don't get woofed by a mega hole or get stuffed under a rock, the rapids are pretty forgiving.

The skill levels required are:
Intermediate to Advanced (open & decked boats) @ ⁻0.6" to 0.6'
advanced-intermediate to expert " " " " @ 0.7" to 1.6'
   expert (open) and advanced-intermediate (decked) @ 1.8'-2.8'
   expert (open and decked)   3.0' & up

* Fayette Station Gauge

For additional information, read Burrell & Davidson's excellent book _Wildwater West Virginia_.

Note: During the tourist season and on weekends & holidays, the lower gorge becomes a zoo from NOON to mid-afternoon. There are so many rafts and boaters thrashing around in there it looks like a disaster movie. (Don't miss Charlton Heston, Ernest Borgnine, George Kennedy, and a host of others in "Raftport 1981"!!)

punching the top wave in Lower Keeney at <u>low</u> water

W. Nealy Photo

Put In
upstream of bridge

Thurm[...]

Since rapid ratings change drastically as the water level goes up, please note high water ratings— seen in parenthesis

Lower Railroad Rapid
Class IV   Mile 8
run left of center over a series of broken ledges. technical below 1', big waves and holes at higher levels. Avoid the steepest drop by sneaking far rt.

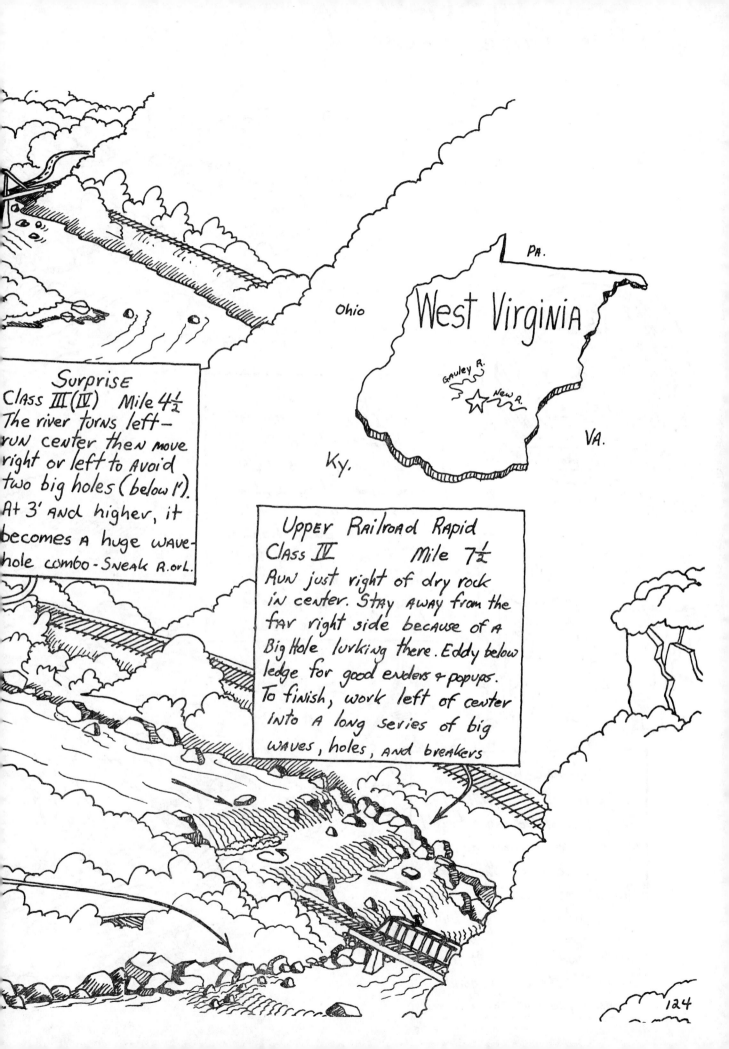

Surprise
Class III(IV)   Mile 4½
The river turns left —
run center then move
right or left to avoid
two big holes (below 1').
At 3' and higher, it
becomes a huge wave-
hole combo - Sneak R. or L.

West Virginia

PA.
Ohio
Gauley R.
New R.
Ky.
VA.

Upper Railroad Rapid
Class IV   Mile 7½
Run just right of dry rock
in center. Stay away from the
far right side because of a
Big Hole lurking there. Eddy below
ledge for good enders & popups.
To finish, work left of center
into a long series of big
waves, holes, and breakers

New River Gorge - Continued

Eskimo Roll (Trad.)

Upper Keeney
Class III (IV)   Mile 9½
(Randy Carter rates it Class V)
Disappointing at 0' or below,
a screamer above 2'. Long
series of big waves—extremely
fast water. Eddy behind
Whale Rock on your left.
Breathe deeply, adjust your
noseplugs and prepare
for the Middle Keeney

Middle Keeney
Class IV (V)   Mile 9⅝
This is what Columbus thought
would happen when he got
to the edge of the world.
Run straight down the center
and, with luck, you will
miss some of the monster
holes and waves. At levels
below 3' there is a good
recovery pool at the bottom

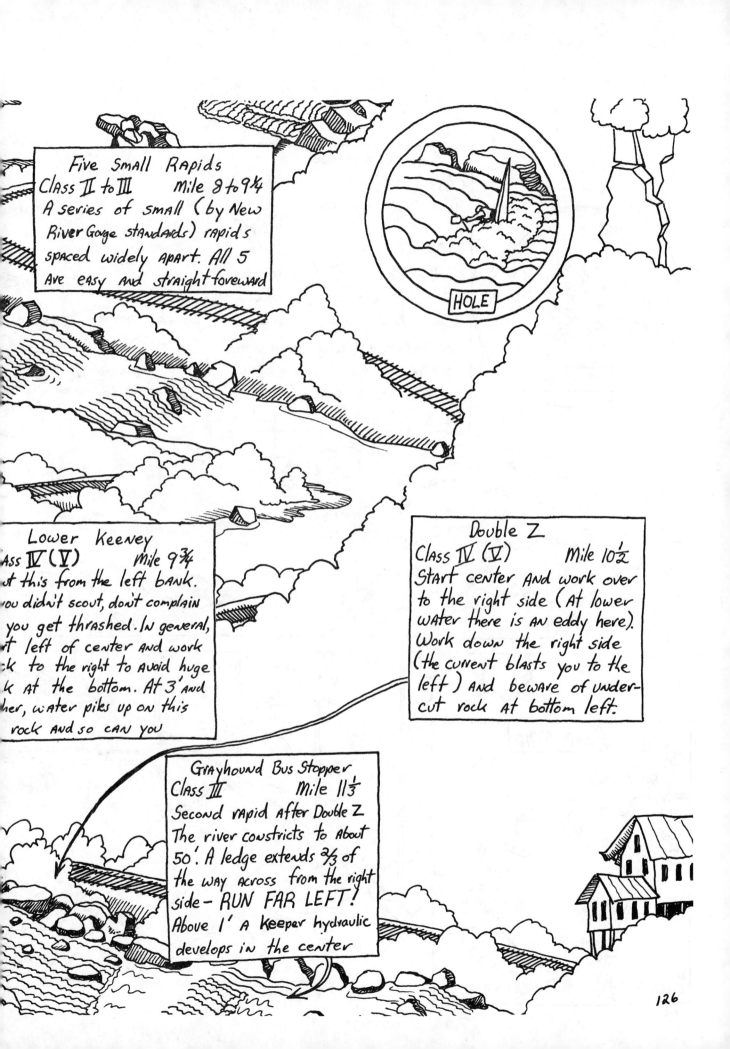

Five Small Rapids
Class II to III   Mile 8 to 9¼
A series of small (by New
River Gorge standards) rapids
spaced widely apart. All 5
are easy and straight foreward

HOLE

Lower Keeney
Ass IV (V)   Mile 9¾
ut this from the left bank.
ou didn't scout, don't complain
you get thrashed. In general,
t left of center and work
ck to the right to avoid huge
k at the bottom. At 3' and
her, water piles up on this
rock and so can you

Double Z
Class IV (V)   Mile 10½
Start center and work over
to the right side (at lower
water there is an eddy here).
Work down the right side
(the current blasts you to the
left) and beware of undercut rock at bottom left.

Grayhound Bus Stopper
Class III   Mile 11⅓
Second rapid after Double Z
The river constricts to about
50'. A ledge extends ⅔ of
the way across from the right
side - RUN FAR LEFT!
Above 1' a keeper hydraulic
develops in the center

126

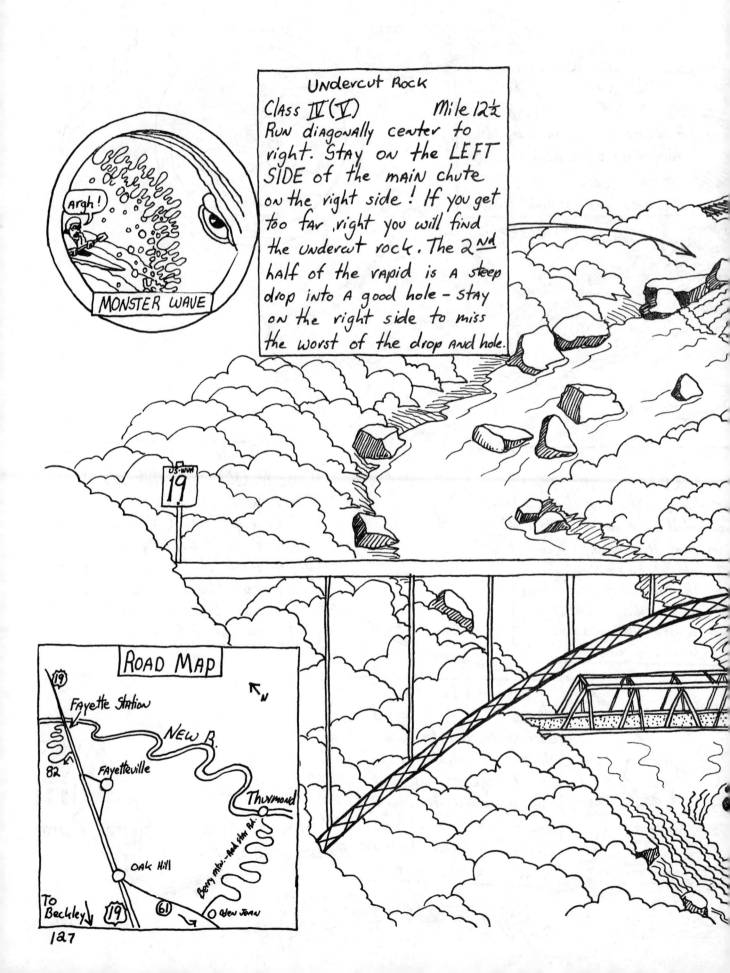

Undercut Rock

Class IV (V)   Mile 12½

Run diagonally center to right. Stay on the LEFT SIDE of the main chute on the right side! If you get too far right you will find the undercut rock. The 2nd half of the rapid is a steep drop into a good hole - stay on the right side to miss the worst of the drop and hole.

Argh!

MONSTER WAVE

US-WVA 19

ROAD MAP

N

19

Fayette Station

NEW R.

82

Fayetteville

Thurmond

Oak Hill

Berry Mtn. - Red Star Rd.

To Beckley

19

61

Glen Jean

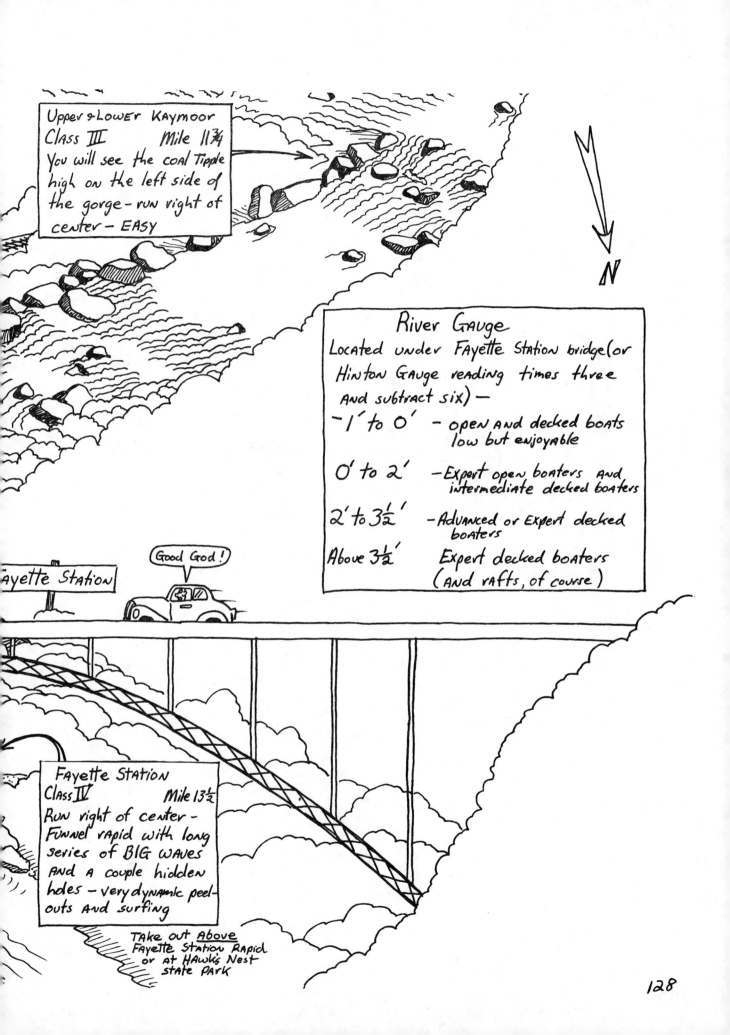

Upper & Lower Kaymoor
Class III   Mile 11¾
You will see the coal Tipple
high on the left side of
the gorge - run right of
center - EASY

N

River Gauge
Located under Fayette Station bridge (or
Hinton Gauge reading times three
And subtract six) —
-1' to 0' - open and decked boats
           low but enjoyable

0' to 2'   - Expert open boaters and
             intermediate decked boaters

2' to 3½' - Advanced or Expert decked
             boaters

Above 3½' Expert decked boaters
           (And rafts, of course)

Good God!

Fayette Station

Fayette Station
Class IV   Mile 13½
Run right of center -
Funnel rapid with long
series of BIG waves
And a couple hidden
holes - very dynamic peel-
outs And surfing

Take out Above
Fayette Station Rapid
or at Hawk's Nest
state Park

128

Nolichucky River

130

Nolichucky River — Continued

The Nolichucky River is formed by the confluence of the Toe and Cane Rivers near the micro-town of Estatoe. Estatoe is named after the daughter of an Indian chief who drowned herself in the Toe R. upon hearing her lover, a member of a rival tribe, had been killed in battle. The area around the Nolichucky was once the mutual hunting ground for the Cherokee and Catawba Indians. When the first Europeans came to the area in the late 17th century, they heard Indian legends about Spanish explorers who mined & smelted the gold & silver in the Toe Cane Valley during the late 15th century. The native Americans were not miners but there is some archeological evidence of mining and smelting operations dating back well over 400 years. There is also corroborative evidence found in the journal of a Spaniard who accompanied Hernando DeSoto on his quest for gold; a quest that definately took DeSoto into North Carolina in 1540. I figure it <u>had</u> to be the Spanish because if aliens had been mining around there, they probably would have left a pyramid or two lying around the Toe Cane Valley. Or some Indian would have spotted the alien spacecrafts and we would have legends about strange creatures from the Dog Star today, not a bunch of mundane legends about some dizzy Spaniards in search of cities of gold.

We do know that mining has been going on in the area continually since the early 17th century. Like all Appalachian mining areas, the Toe Cane Valley has lots of stories to tell about fortunes found & fortunes lost, with lots of blood shed along the way. Muriel Sheppard's excellent book, <u>Cabins In the Laurel</u>, contains lots of sordid details about the seamy side (and the good side) of life in the mountains. Highly recommended reading!

Today, railroads and trains are the most salient feature around the Nolichucky. When the Clinchfield RR was being constructed late in the last century, the contract for the building of the gorge section of the tracks was being hotly contested. The two competing companies decided to race from Huntdale, N.C., to the mouth of the gorge. Whoever built the railbed that far <u>first</u> got the contract. To this day, remains of the loser's railbed can be found on the west side of the river, across from Poplar, N.C..

The put in is in 'lower' Poplar, N.C.. Take Indian Grave Gap Rd. (Class IV-V wet or dry) into Erwin, TN.. Go south on 19-w/23 to the bridge, then left to the take out at Unaka Springs. Erwin is a strange place. In the 20's, the townsfolk lynched (of all things) a circus elephant that had accidentally squashed a child. Not having a strong enough rope, they used a crane mounted on a RR flatcar to do the deed. Ripley's Believe It or Not put Erwin on the map for this fascinating bit of countryfied jurisprudence. Erwin is also famous for it's Nuclear fuels reprocessing plant. The N.R.C. figured a bunch of out-of-work moonshiners were just the ticket for plutonium recovery operations. Over a period of a few years the plant managed to "lose" 90 lbs. of enriched weapons-grade plutonium oxide, so the N.R.C. reluctantly shut them down. If you happen to find 90 lbs. of plutonium lying around, call the mayor of Erwin - there's probably a reward!

The Nolichucky Gorge is one of North Carolina's best whitewater runs. Catching it at a good level is the only real problem. It's usually too low or too high, with only a 1.5' water level tolerence between minimum and maximum running levels. Please do not attempt to run this river above 3.1' - it is extremely dangerous! The gradient averages between 48-66 feet per mile for the first two miles. It "lets up" to a stately 36 f.p.m. for the lower 7.5 miles. The gorge winds through the Cherokee National Forest, with Bald & Flattop mountains on the left and the Unaka Mountains on the right. If you look carefully, high on the right-hand slopes you may glimpse rubble piles below some old mica mines. Runoff from the many mine rubble piles in the area makes the Nolichucky slightly radioactive, but it's no more dangerous than driving through Harrisburg, Pennsylvania.

At the North Carolina - Tennessee state line (mile 5.9) stop and hike up Devil's Creek (on the left). There is a good trail running up the righthand side of the creek. It takes you to a waterfall and grotto that are quite beautiful.

The Gorge - Poplar, N.C. To Unaka Springs, T

Railroad Bridge Rapid - Class III -
As you pass beneath the RR trestle, you'll probably
notice things begin to pick up rather abruptly...
Stay rt. of center and watch for two holes
bottom left. This is a screamer
above 2.9'....

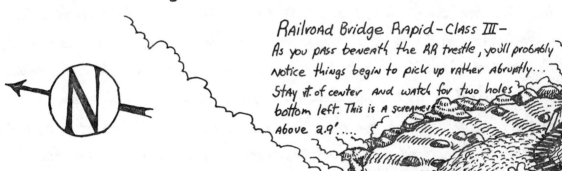

On The Rocks - III-IV (IV) - You encounter
this aptly named rapid just after "RR.
Bridge Rapid's" pool... Scout from the
left bank. Theoretically, you run the
4' drop rt. to l. on the tongue
thus avoiding two holes at the
bottom. <u>Immediately</u> go right
(two chutes) or left to avoid
a large, poorly padded boulder..
followed by more of the same.
Consequences: holes, rocks,
strainers, broken boats/craniums,
etc.

"Loner"
Class III -

Unaka Mountains

ROOSTERTAIL

Roostertail - Class III (III-III) The name of this rapid is a
misnomer because the roostertail-rock washed away a few years back.
Begin right then work left after the big drop. Eddy right for gre
enders & dynamic peelouts. (you need a FAST roll here as head-h
-rock in 4 seconds). End left of the big rock bottom-center. Ab
2.8', run rt. of center and stay in the long series of big standin
waves - it looks like you're going to get washed onto the rock
but the current shoves you left. Nice play spot at the bottom.

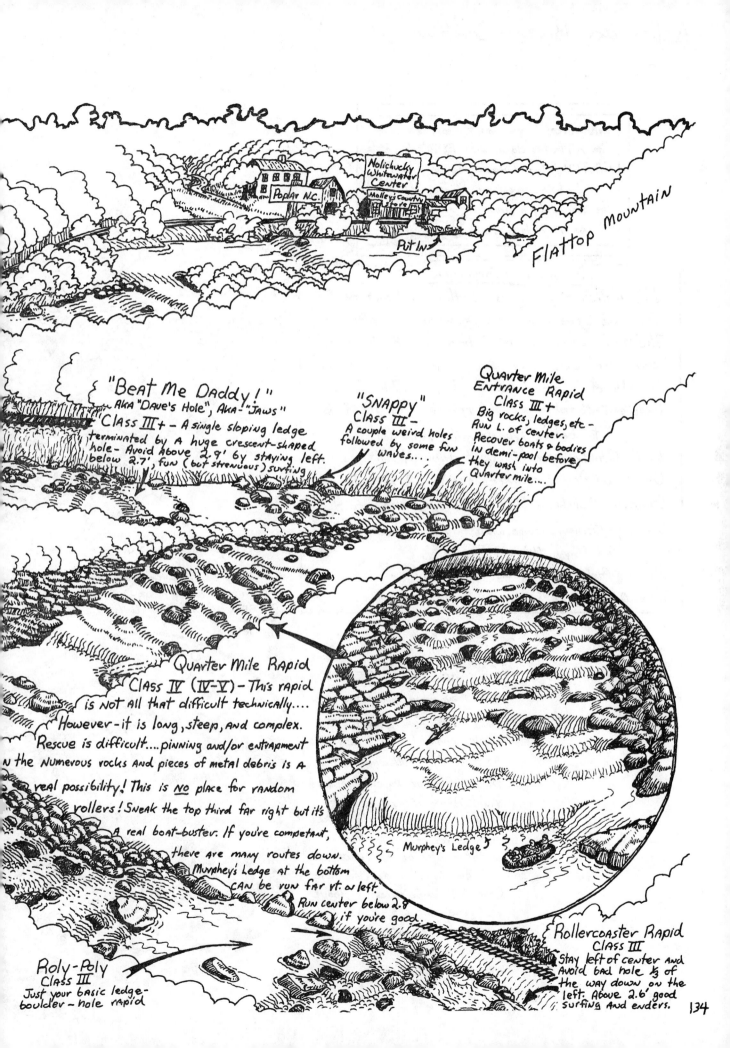

Nolichucky Whitewater Center

Poplar N.C.

Molley's County Store

Put In

Flattop Mountain

"Beat Me Daddy!"
Aka "Dave's Hole", Aka "Jaws"
Class III+ - A single sloping ledge terminated by a huge crescent-shaped hole - Avoid above 2.9' by staying left. below 2.7', fun (but strenuous) surfing

"Snappy"
Class III-
A couple weird holes followed by some fun waves....

Quarter Mile Entrance Rapid
Class III+
Big rocks, ledges, etc - Run L. of center. Recover boats & bodies in demi-pool before they wash into Quarter mile....

Quarter Mile Rapid
Class IV (IV-V) - This rapid is not all that difficult technically.... However - it is long, steep, and complex. Rescue is difficult....pinning and/or entrapment in the numerous rocks and pieces of metal debris is a real possibility! This is NO place for random rollers! Sneak the top third far right but it's a real boat-buster. If you're competant, there are many routes down. Murphey's Ledge at the bottom can be run far rt. or left. Run center below 2.8 if you're good.

Murphey's Ledge

Roly-Poly
Class III
Just your basic ledge-boulder-hole rapid

Rollercoaster Rapid
Class III
Stay left of center and avoid bad hole ⅓ of the way down on the left. Above 2.6' good surfing and enders.

134

Nolichucky River — Continued

General Information

The Nolichucky begins at the confluence of the Toe and Cane Rivers 3.5 miles above Poplar, N.C. The Gorge begins .6 miles below the Put-In and continues until mile 8.

Length of Trip - 9 miles   (4½ - 7 hours)

Gradient - 36 feet per mile - 66 f.p.m from "On the Rocks" to below Quartermile Rapid!

Water Quality - fair (ie: don't drink it...)

Overall difficulty rating - Class IV (2.5' to 3.2')

Geology - "Nolichucky Shale", sandstone, mica, etc.

Scenery - Excellent! Gorge winds thru the Unaka Mountains and Pisgah National Forest -

Put In - Poplar, N.C.   (see Road map)

Take Out - Unaka Springs RR Trestle (see map)

mile 4

Rock Garden Rapid
Class III
300 yds of technical stuff terminated by a mega-pile of boulders - A real boat-buster below 2.7' - carry far left.

SOUSEHOLE

Maggie's Rock

Hole

"Sousehole" - Class III - half a mile below Sycamore Shoals the river divides into two channels - The center channel is dry below 3.5' so, obviously, you'll want to take the narrow, curving channel far right. After 150 yds of fast water you will hopefully notice a large rock - "Maggie's Rock" - in the center of the flow. Run left and into the dreaded hole (see Bob Benner's desc.). Above 2.7' the hole washes out and a series of impressive waves forms - Run sideways or backwards for maximum enjoyment.

135

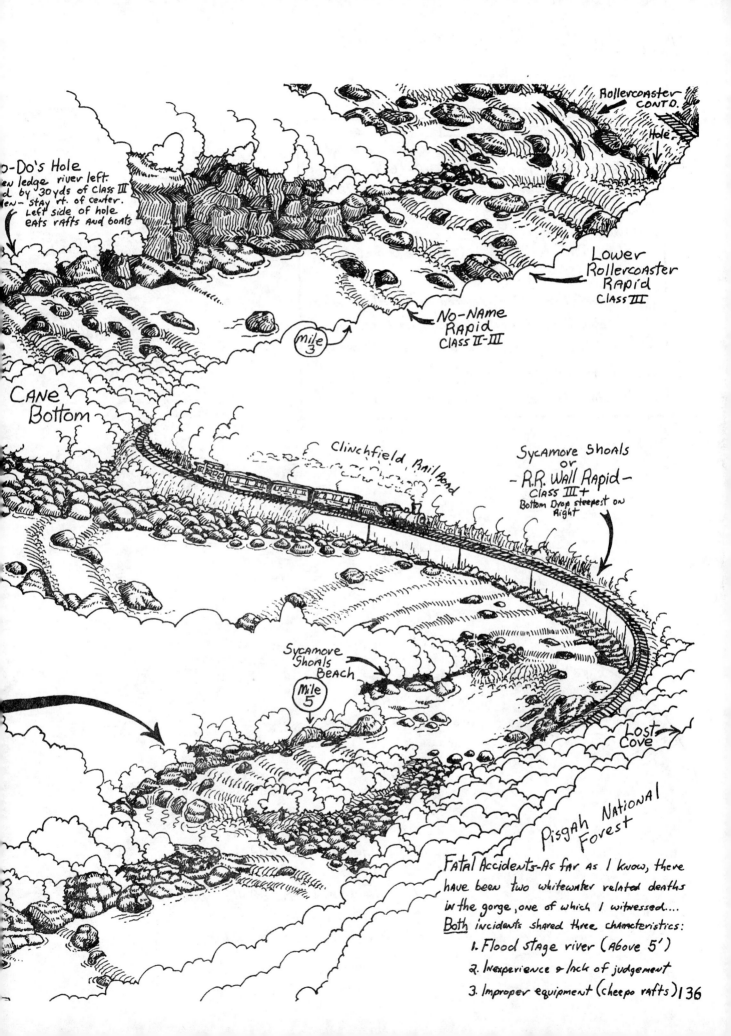

Rollercoaster
CONT'D.

Hole

Lower
Rollercoaster
Rapid
Class III

o-Do's Hole
en ledge river left.
d by 30yds of Class II
en- stay rt. of center.
Left side of hole
eats rafts and boats

No-Name
Rapid
Class II-III

mile 3

Cane
Bottom

Clinchfield Railroad

Sycamore Shoals
or
- R.R. Wall Rapid -
Class III+
Bottom Drop steepest on
Right

Sycamore
Shoals
Beach

Mile 5

Lost
Cove

Pisgah National Forest

Fatal Accidents - As far as I know, there
have been two whitewater related deaths
in the gorge, one of which I witnessed....
Both incidents shared three characteristics:

1. Flood stage river (Above 5')

2. Inexperience & lack of judgement

3. Improper equipment (cheepo rafts) 136

Nolichucky River - Continued

Tennessee State Line

Mile 6

Big Eddy

Appalachian Trail

Shoo-fly Shoals
- Technical class III -
fun above 2.2'
Real bitch below 1.8'

Nolichucky Expeditions Inc.

The Slide - class rollercoaster ride on series of standing w...

The Artist: Paddling The Susquehanna...below 3 mile Island Nuclear Plant

"Night paddling is easy...when you glow in the dark!"

This map is dedicated to my friends, Gail Kirchner and Jimm East...

Thanks and a tip of the 'yak to: Rick Murray, Mike Mayfield, John Regan, Virgil & Jenny, and Diff Ritchie.

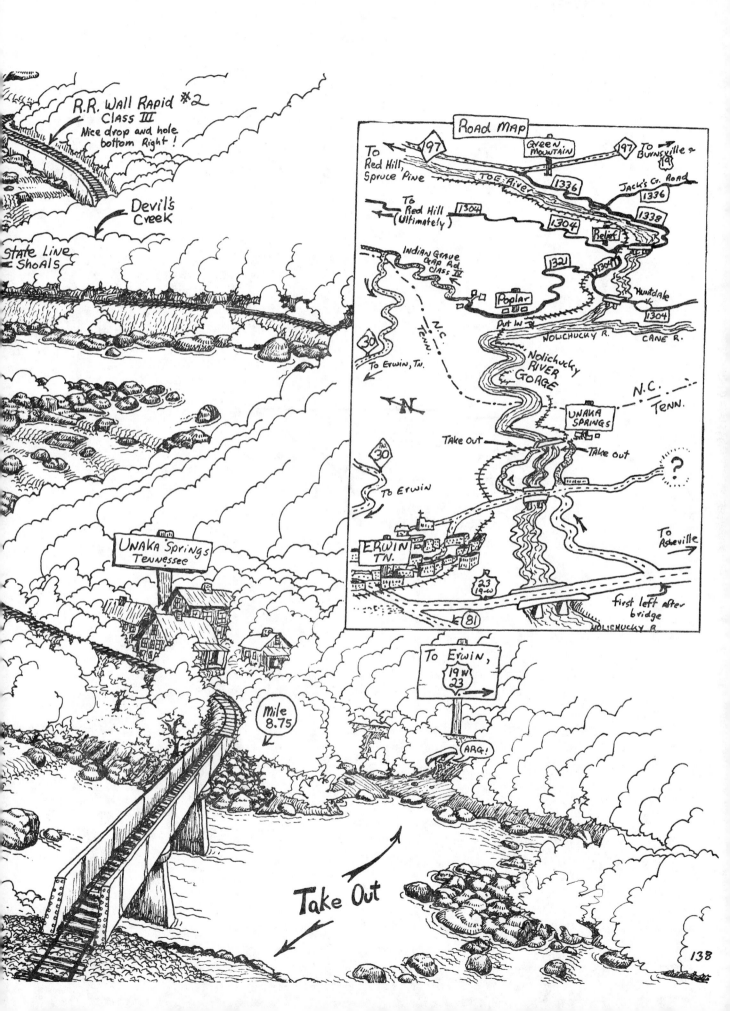

R.R. Wall Rapid #2
Class III
Nice drop and hole
bottom Right !

Devil's Creek

State Line Shoals

Unaka Springs Tennessee

mile 8.75

Take Out

Road Map

To Red Hill, Spruce Pine

To Red Hill (Ultimately)

Green Mountain

To Burnsville

Toe River

Jack's Cr. Road

Relief

Indian Grave Gap Rd. Class IV

Poplar

Huntdale

Put In

Nolichucky R.

Cane R.

To Erwin, Tn.

N.C. Tenn.

Nolichucky RIVER GORGE

Take Out

Unaka Springs

Take Out

N.C. Tenn.

To Erwin

?

Erwin Tn.

To Asheville

first left after bridge

Nolichucky R.

To Erwin, 19 W 23

ARG!

138

Ocoee River

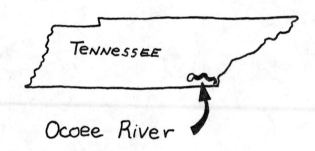

Ocoee River

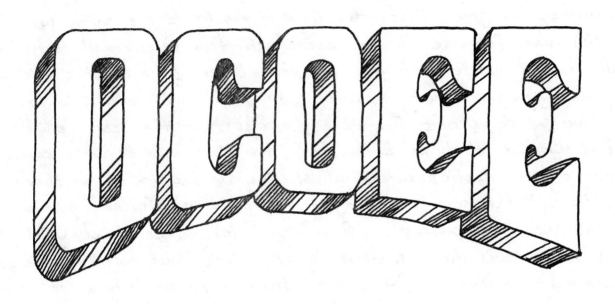

Ocoee River-Continued

The controversy surrounding the future of this outstanding whitewater river is as bizzare as any of the Ocoee's many rapids. After decades of being a dry riverbed, the Ocoee began running a few years back when the wooden flume feeding the #2 powerhouse broke. For a while it looked as if the flume would be abandoned altogether and the Ocoee would run free for good. Alas, the T.V.A. (thanks to the canny use of ancient alchemical formulae on the cost-benefit figures) decided to rebuild after all. Always astute apologists for pork-barrel projects, the T.V.A. is currently engaged in a not-to-secret war with outfitters and boaters over the future of the Ocoee. Forgetting the fact that the Ocoee attracts hundreds of thousands of dollars to the area*, the T.V.A. has begun a campaig of economic scare tactics aimed at stirring up the locals so they will smite (literally) the evil outside agitators (paddlers). Already blaming us for rate increases (present and future) and loss of construction jobs, the T.V.A. has drawn the battle-lines clearly. Hope those outfitters have good fire insurance — welcome to the O.M.Z. Help us in our holy quest against the loathsome leviathan, T.V.A. — Write to the Ocoee River Council, c/o David Brown, Rt.1, Ocoee, TN, 37361!

The Ocoee is one of the Southeast's greatest whitewater runs! It's 57 foot per mile gradient creates over six miles of non-stop Class III-IV rapids. Most of the rapids are of the drop-pool variety, with very little "pool" to speak of. Though few of the rapids are rated above Class III-IV, they are crammed together so closely that the overall rating is Class IV. Above 3,500 cfs the river takes on a Class IV-V persona. Skill levels required are: intermediate to advanced open & decked boaters up to 1650 cfs, Advanced intermediate to expert up to 2,600 cfs (with trepidation). Experts (open & decked boat) up to 3,500 cfs. Eskimo rolls and self-rescue (open boaters) are fundamental skills necessary to the enjoyment of this river

* per year

A couple years back I watched some crazy friends run the Ocoee at 16,000 cfs, from below Double Suck to the take out. The big rock at Diamond Splitter was completely submerged and they nearly got clotheslined on slalom-gate suspension wires at Powerhouse Rapid (the wires were even with the bottom of the bridge!). The worst rapid appeared just upstream of the take out (where no rapid exists) where the fast watr hit the lake and shot skyward in a series of 10'-12' offset exploding waves.

Ocoee River - Continued

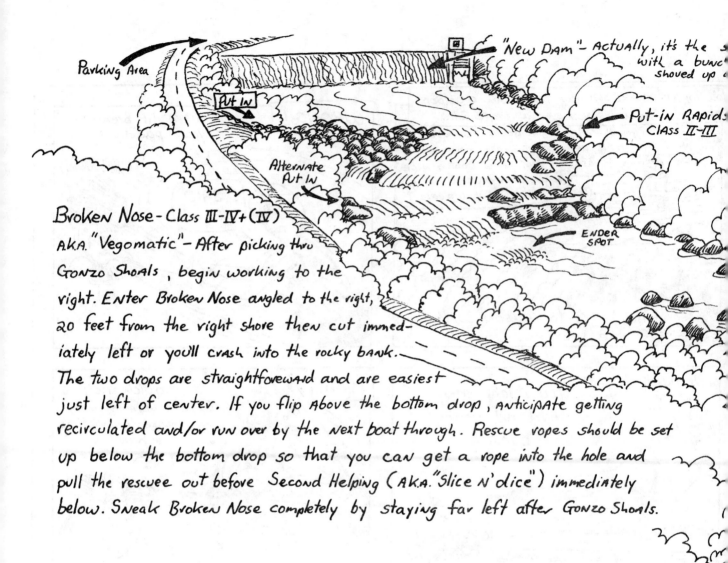

Parking Area

PUT IN

Alternate Put In

"New Dam" - Actually, it's the s...
with a bunc...
shoved up...

Put-in Rapids
CLASS II-III

ENDER SPOT

Broken Nose - Class III-IV+ (IV)
A.K.A. "Vegomatic" - After picking thru
Gonzo Shoals, begin working to the
right. Enter Broken Nose angled to the right,
20 feet from the right shore then cut immediately left or you'll crash into the rocky bank.
The two drops are straightforeward and are easiest
just left of center. If you flip above the bottom drop, anticipate getting
recirculated and/or run over by the next boat through. Rescue ropes should be set
up below the bottom drop so that you can get a rope into the hole and
pull the rescuee out before Second Helping (A.K.A. "Slice n' dice") immediately
below. Sneak Broken Nose completely by staying far left after Gonzo Shoals.

Double Suck - Class III-IV - A.K.A. "Turkeys left,
heroes right" - preceeded by 50-60 yds of
Class II-III ledge-shoal stuff. Run just right
of the big rock, down the drop & into the
first hole....then left or right to avoid the
bad hidden hole just below. Sneak- far
right or far left of the big rock. Note-the
hidden hole looks small but it can gobble
you and your boat whole. There's a good
rescue-eddy on the left after the drop. Watch
for the new bridge piling 70' below.

Double Suck
Class III-IV

SNEAK

or

Hidden hole

Gonzo Shoals - Class III
A long obstructed boulder-
ledge garden with lots of
small drops and technical
routes. Good luck!

Broken Nose
Class III - IV +

Right
Bank

G

G

2nd Drop - 3'

3rd Drop

Second Helping - class III -
A bizzare jumble of rocks
holes, broken ledges and
fast water. Go far left after
Broken Nose.

MOON
Shoot

Chicken
Route

New
Bridge

144

Ocoee River - Continued

★ Diamond Splitter - Class III-IV (A.K.A. "8-ball") Immediately below the micro-pool at the bottom of Tablesaw, the river plunges over a series of drops with a monolithic rock bisecting the channel. Run this by working far right just after Tablesaw. Stay to the right of the giant rock for a great series of waves. Eddy right or left (best) below. If you run to the left of the rock, prepare for a bumpy ride over shallow ledges ending in "Hollywood Hole"—a particularly violent & grabby hole bottom-center. Hollywood is great for surfing, if you like epic surfing. The hole loves C-boats particularly, but will eat anything. While Tablesaw starts washing out at 2,600 cfs, Diamond Splitter gets meaner and merges with the rapids below to create a quarter mile of III-IV water. Rough on swimmers, needless to say.

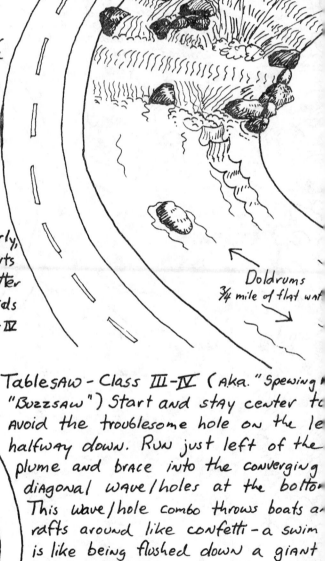

Doldrums
3/4 mile of flat wat...

Diamond Splitter
Class III-IV

watch for hole at the bottom if you run left of the rock.

Class III entrance rapid

or...

Big Hole

Pyramidical Breaking wave

Tablesaw - Class III-IV (aka. "Spewing ... "Buzzsaw") Start and stay center to avoid the troublesome hole on the le... halfway down. Run just left of the plume and brace into the converging diagonal wave/holes at the botto... This wave/hole combo throws boats a... rafts around like confetti—a swim... is like being flushed down a giant toilet. Eddy left and rescue swimme... immediately—Diamond Splitter is just be...

huh?

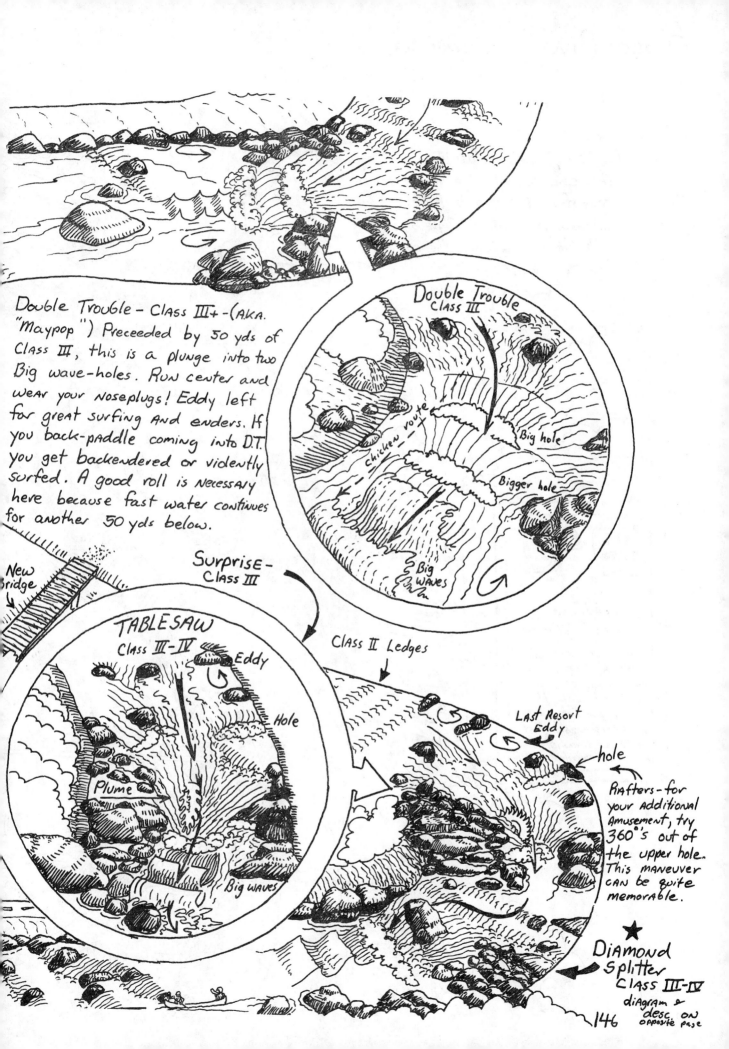

Double Trouble Class III

Double Trouble – Class III+ – (A.K.A. "Maypop") Preceeded by 50 yds of Class III, this is a plunge into two Big wave-holes. Run center and wear your Noseplugs! Eddy left for great surfing and enders. If you back-paddle coming into D.T. you get backendered or violently surfed. A good roll is necessary here because fast water continues for another 50 yds below.

chicken route

Big hole

Bigger hole

Big waves

G

New Bridge

Surprise – Class III

TABLESAW Class III-IV

Eddy

Hole

Plume

Big Waves

Class II Ledges

Last Resort Eddy

hole

Rafters – for your additional amusement, try 360's out of the upper hole. This maneuver can be quite memorable.

★ Diamond Splitter Class III-IV diagram & desc. on opposite page

Ocoee River - Continued

Cat's Pyjamas - Class III + (A.K.A. "Torpedo")
This challenging little rapid looks
easy from the top but gets crazy
toward the bottom. Right of center
all the way down is the easiest
route.

Headgear
Anyone paddling on
this river **should**
wear a helmet. The
Abundance of rocks
combined with the
swift current create
A serious hazard that
should be taken into
Account by competant paddlers

Raft Trips
Nantahala outdoor
center — ocoee
outpost
TVA Recording
615-525-5751
Ocoee, Tn.

Ocoee INN
FOOD!

US 64

Shoulder Parking

Shoulder Parking

O Nice day
for something...

Take Out ¼ mile
downstream
on the
right

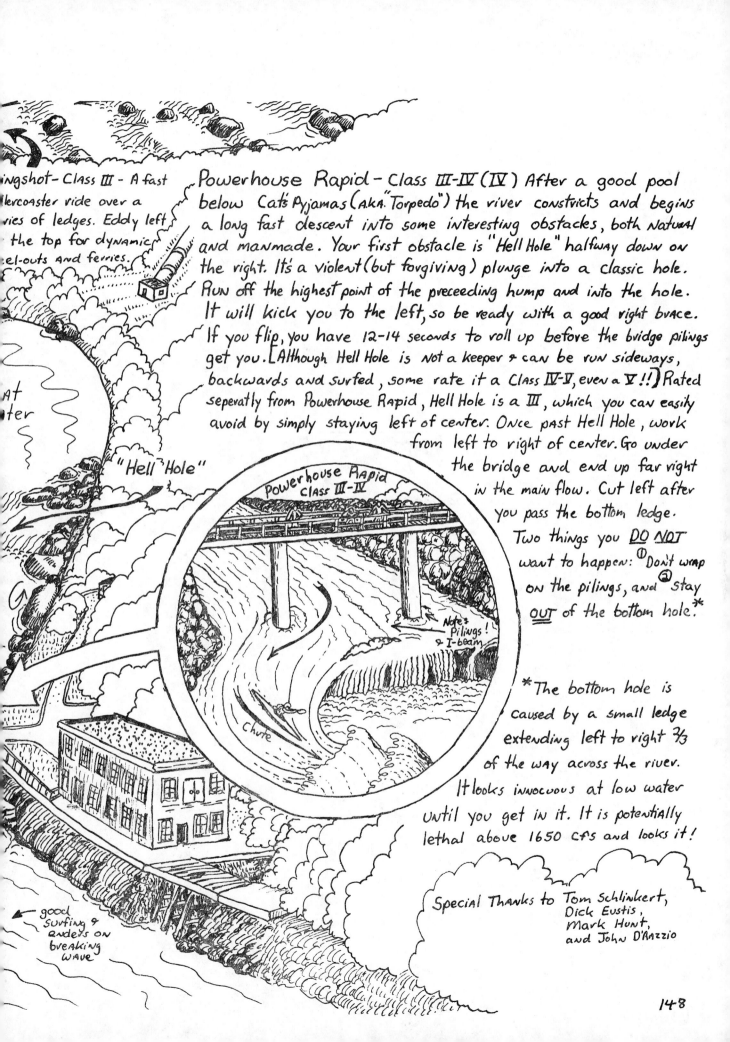

ingshot- Class III - A fast
llercoaster ride over a
ries of ledges. Eddy left
the top for dynamic
el-outs and ferries.

Powerhouse Rapid – Class III-IV (IV) After a good pool below Cat's Pyjamas (a.k.a. "Torpedo") the river constricts and begins a long fast descent into some interesting obstacles, both Natural and manmade. Your first obstacle is "Hell Hole" halfway down on the right. It's a violent (but forgiving) plunge into a classic hole. Run off the highest point of the preceeding hump and into the hole. It will kick you to the left, so be ready with a good right brace. If you flip, you have 12-14 seconds to roll up before the bridge pilings get you. [Although Hell Hole is not a keeper & can be run sideways, backwards and surfed, some rate it a Class IV-V, even a V !!] Rated seperatly from Powerhouse Rapid, Hell Hole is a III, which you can easily avoid by simply staying left of center. Once past Hell Hole, work from left to right of center. Go under the bridge and end up far right in the main flow. Cut left after you pass the bottom ledge.

Two things you DO NOT want to happen: ① Don't wrap on the pilings, and ② Stay OUT of the bottom hole.*

"Hell" Hole"

Powerhouse Rapid
Class III-IV

Note:
Pilings!
& I-beam

Chute

*The bottom hole is caused by a small ledge extending left to right 2/3 of the way across the river. It looks innocuous at low water until you get in it. It is potentially lethal above 1650 cfs and looks it!

good surfing & enders on breaking wave

Special Thanks to Tom Schlinkert, Dick Eustis, Mark Hunt, and John D'Razzio

Savage River

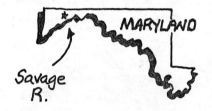

Savage R.

MARYLAND

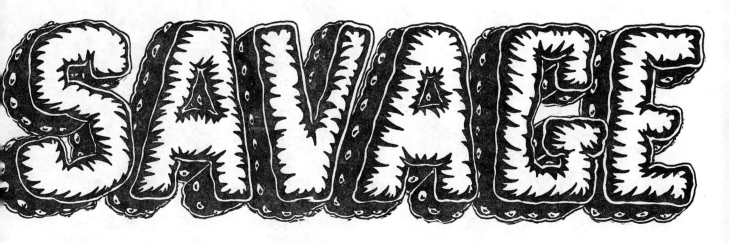

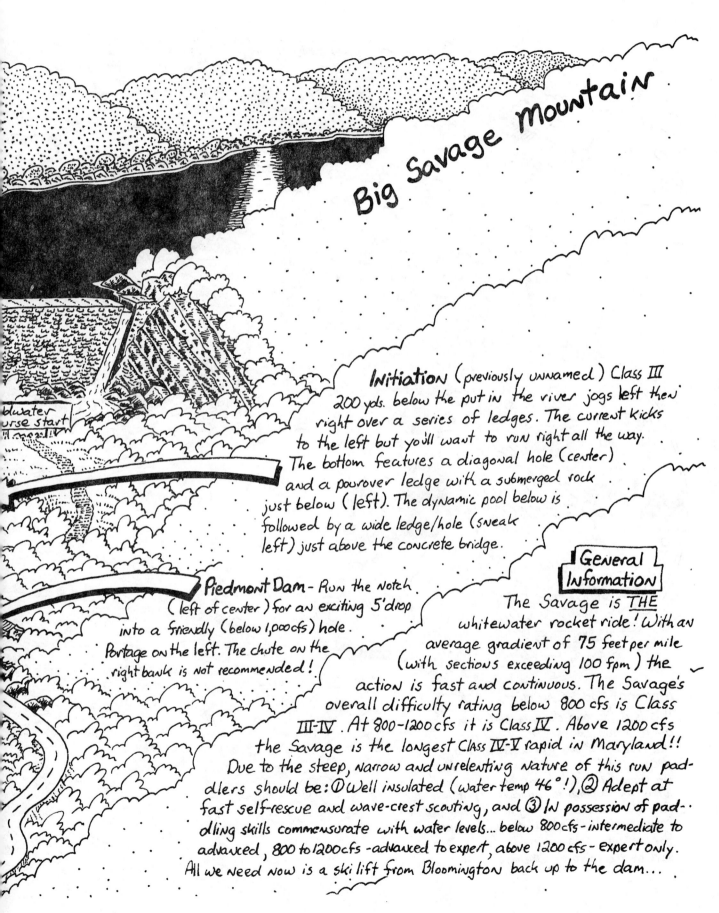

Big Savage Mountain

dwater
urse start

Initiation (previously unnamed) Class III
200 yds. below the put in the river jogs left then
right over a series of ledges. The current kicks
to the left but you'll want to run right all the way.
The bottom features a diagonal hole (center)
and a pourover ledge with a submerged rock
just below (left). The dynamic pool below is
followed by a wide ledge/hole (sneak
left) just above the concrete bridge.

Piedmont Dam - Run the notch
(left of center) for an exciting 5'drop
into a friendly (below 1,000 cfs) hole.
Portage on the left. The chute on the
right bank is not recommended!

General Information

The Savage is **THE**
whitewater rocket ride! With an
average gradient of 75 feet per mile
(with sections exceeding 100 fpm) the
action is fast and continuous. The Savage's
overall difficulty rating below 800 cfs is Class
III-IV. At 800-1200 cfs it is Class IV. Above 1200 cfs
the Savage is the longest Class IV-V rapid in Maryland!!
Due to the steep, narrow and unrelenting nature of this run paddlers should be: ① Well insulated (water temp 46°!), ② Adept at
fast self-rescue and wave-crest scouting, and ③ In possession of paddling skills commensurate with water levels... below 800 cfs-intermediate to
advanced, 800 to 1200 cfs -advanced to expert, above 1200 cfs - expert only.
All we need now is a ski lift from Bloomington back up to the dam...

152

Savage R., cont'd.

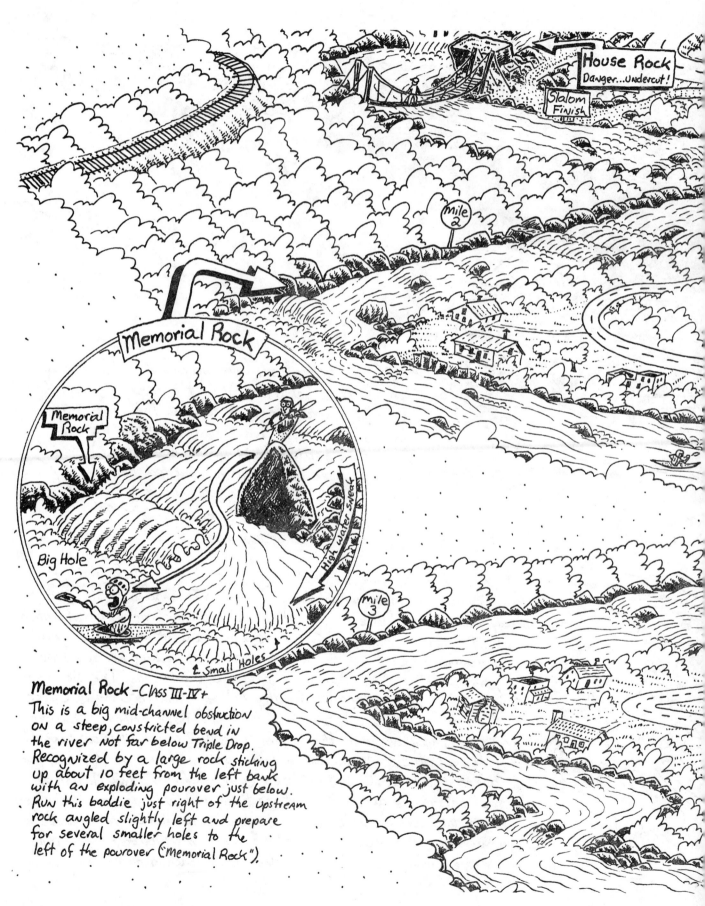

Memorial Rock - Class III-IV+
This is a big mid-channel obstruction
on a steep, constricted bend in
the river not far below Triple Drop.
Recognized by a large rock sticking
up about 10 feet from the left bank
with an exploding pourover just below.
Run this baddie just right of the upstream
rock angled slightly left and prepare
for several smaller holes to the
left of the pourover ("Memorial Rock").

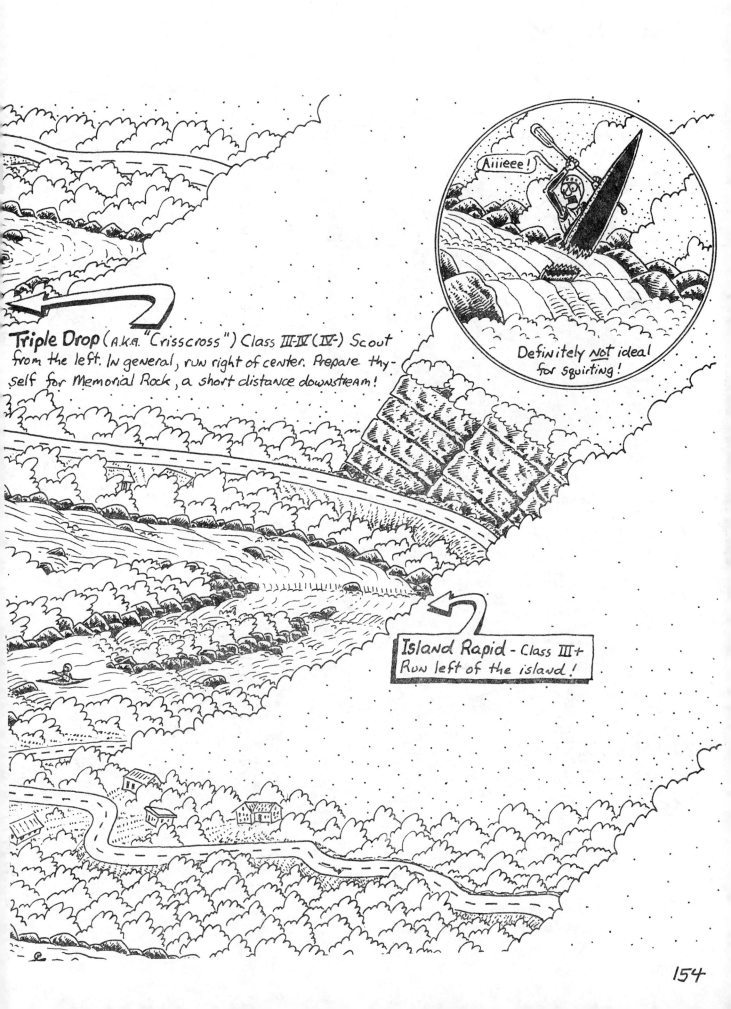

Triple Drop (A.K.A. "Crisscross") Class III-IV (IV-) Scout from the left. In general, run right of center. Prepare thyself for Memorial Rock, a short distance downstream!

Aiiieee!

Definitely **not** ideal for squirting!

Island Rapid - Class III+ Run left of the island!

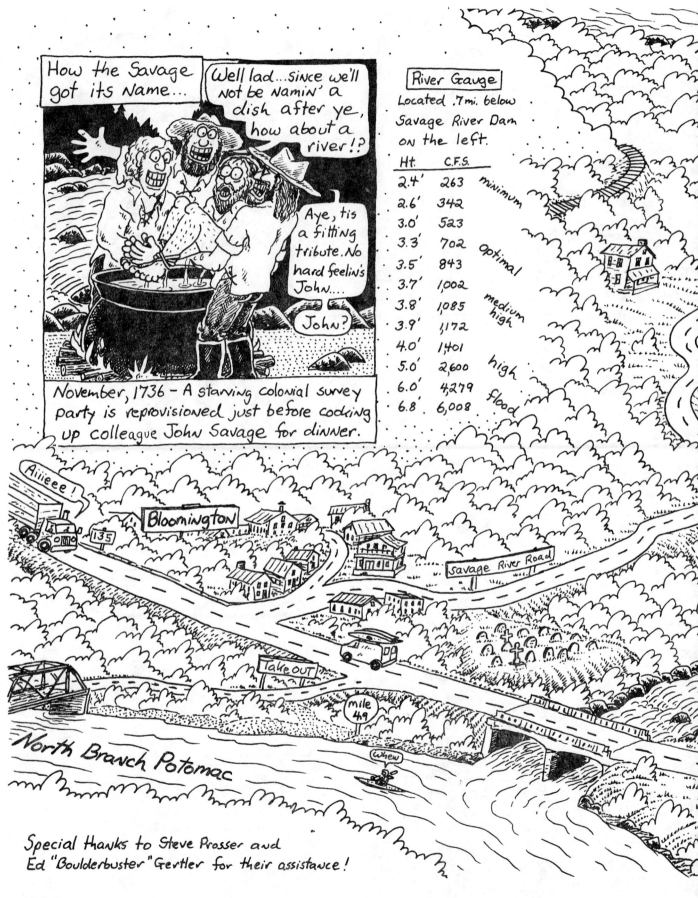

How the Savage got its Name...

Well lad...since we'll not be namin' a dish after ye, how about a river!?

Aye, 'tis a fitting tribute. No hard feelin's John....

John?

November, 1736 — A starving colonial survey party is reprovisioned just before cooking up colleague John Savage for dinner.

River Gauge

Located .7 mi. below Savage River Dam on the left.

Ht.	C.F.S.	
2.4'	263	minimum
2.6'	342	
3.0'	523	
3.3'	702	optimal
3.5'	843	
3.7'	1,002	
3.8'	1,085	medium high
3.9'	1,172	
4.0'	1,401	
5.0'	2,600	high
6.0'	4,279	flood
6.8'	6,008	

Aiiieee!

Bloomington

135

Savage River Road

Take Out

mile 49

Whew

North Branch Potomac

Special thanks to Steve Prosser and Ed "Boulderbuster" Gertler for their assistance!

Youghiogheny River

Pennsylvania

Youghiogheny River

lower
Yough

Youghiogheny River - Continued

Ohiopyle Falls has been run... successfully on several occasions... by wild & crazy (AND EXPERT) decked boaters. It is presently illegal to attempt the falls. Besides, it's extremely dangerous!!

Wilderness Voyageurs Inc.

OHIOPYLE

381

Entrance Rapid

Sugarloaf Rock

Entrance Rapid - Class III-IV - This is the first and one of the best rapids on the loop. It is ⅛ mile long and pretty technical. Start center and work left to avoid Sugarloaf Rock. Entrance offers twisting drops, bizzare crosscurrents and abrupt eddies on both sides. Great at higher levels - huge irregular waves, insane cross-currents, and powerful water. Again, at any level, try not to get painted onto Sugarloaf. Sneak - eddy-hop down the right side - very technical boulder garden-ledge route. (dotted line - diagram)

LOOP TAKEOUT

Loop Takeout Trail - The ¼ mile trail takes you over the old Western Maryland R.R. railbed thru a lovely area known locally as Ferncliff. There are numerous state-maintained trails on the loop for hikers & picnicers.

MILE 2

WESTERN MARYLAND RAILROAD

Railr Rapid -

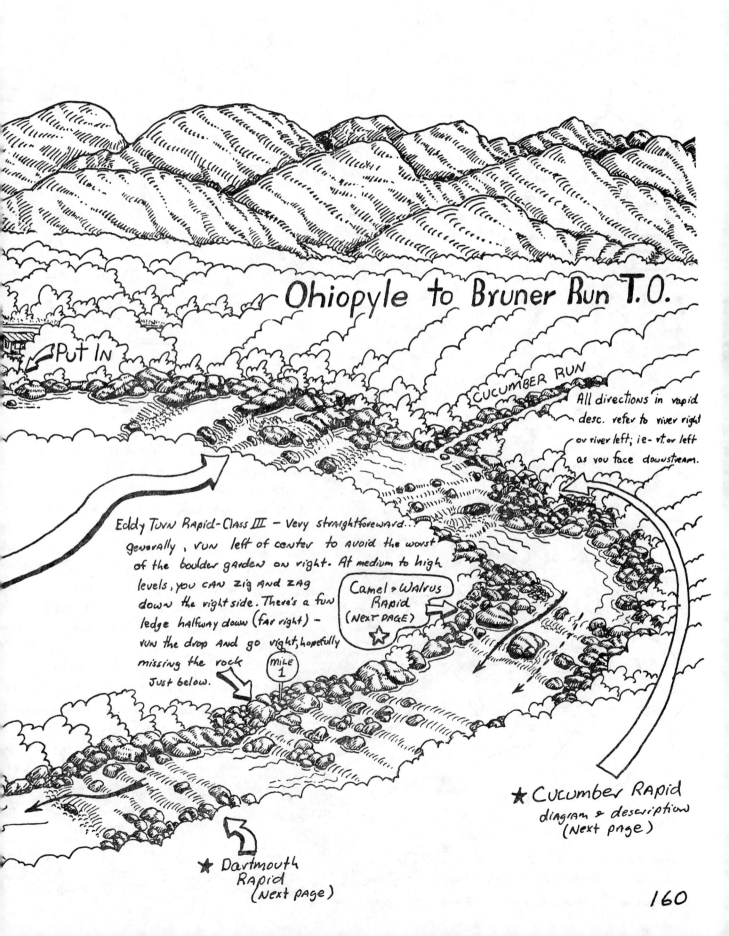

Ohiopyle to Bruner Run T.O.

Put In

CUCUMBER RUN

All directions in rapid desc. refer to river right or river left; ie- rt. or left as you face downstream.

Eddy Turn Rapid - Class III - Very straightforeward... generally, run left of center to avoid the worst of the boulder garden on right. At medium to high levels, you can zig and zag down the right side. There's a fun ledge halfway down (far right) - run the drop and go right, hopefully missing the rock just below.

Camel & Walrus Rapid (NEXT PAGE)

MILE 1

★ Cucumber Rapid
diagram & description
(Next page)

★ Dartmouth Rapid (Next page)

160

Youghiogheny River - Continued

Jim Run

Railroad Rapid - Class III-IV - By the time you spot the RR bridge downstream, you'll be practically on top of the drop. Run center to avoid Charlie's Washingmachine (right) and a diagonal hole (left). After the drop, immediately go right or left to avoid a minefield of rocks just below. (you can run straight at high levels) Decked boats can squeeze thru a weird slot far right for a variation. On the right bank just below is the Loop Take-out - climb the embankment (ugh!) and carry ¼ mile to the parking area.

mile 3

Stulls Run

Three Sisters Rapid

Bear Run

RAILROAD RAPID

weird slot

CHARLIE'S Washingmachine

OR

MAIN FLOW

Dimple

Pinball Rock

High-water sneak

Dimple Rock - Class III-IV - recognized by a gravel bar on the right bank above the rapid. The river gets squeezed left, down, and straight into Dimple Rock. This is the most dangerous spot on the river! Dimple Rock is under cut and two fatalities have occurred here. Head straight for Dimple rock and draw right to miss it. If you wr on Dimple Rock, lean <u>downstream</u>, in the rock and climb onto it. Below Dimple, work right of center and pick your way thru 100 yds of Class III stuff on a curve to the left. Decked boaters will enjoy hopping f Pinball rock eddy to Ⓐ (diagram), unless they f

Dimple ROCK

Ⓐ

Swimmers hole

N

161

Swimmers Rapid - Class II -
Just below Dimple you'll run into a large hole extending ⅔ across the river from the left. Great surfing!

★ Dartmouth Rapid - Class III - The annual Fall Slalom Races are held on this rapid. It's a long boulder garden with lots of weird (but small) ledges thrown in. Run center, then go right at the bottom drop to avoid a submerged rock in the center below the drop. This washes out at higher levels with medium-size standing waves at the bottom.

CUCUMBER
CLASS III-IV

Cucumber Rapid - Class III-IV - Named for Cucumber Run which enters left just upstream. Pick your way down the left side and scout left. Run the double drop center just right of a semi-submerged rock in the middle (diagram). Brace thru the confused holes below the drops, staying in the chute, then out. Running the drop-holes has been compared to being flushed down a toilet. At higher levels, you can run the chute left of the big rock (dotted line-diagram) <u>Scout</u> this rapid!

☆ Camel & Walrus Rapid - Class III - (Next rapid after Cucumber) This is a ledge-boulder rapid that funnels down towards the bottom. To add to our enjoyment, the river gods placed a large boulder-heap at the bottom center. You'll want to avoid it by running right (low to medium level) or left at higher water levels (dotted line).

BOTTLE OF WINE

Pinning rock

Dynamic Eddy

High Water

Johnathan Run

Sugar Run

Bottle of Wine Rapid (A.K.A.-Johns Hopkins) Class III - Run rt. of center and take the rt. chute halfway down. Rafters - Avoid pinning rock on right! At higher levels you can run the left chute, then go far right just below the drop, there's a dynamic eddy on the right At higher levels, there are excellent surfing waves below the chute.

162

Youghiogheny River - Continued

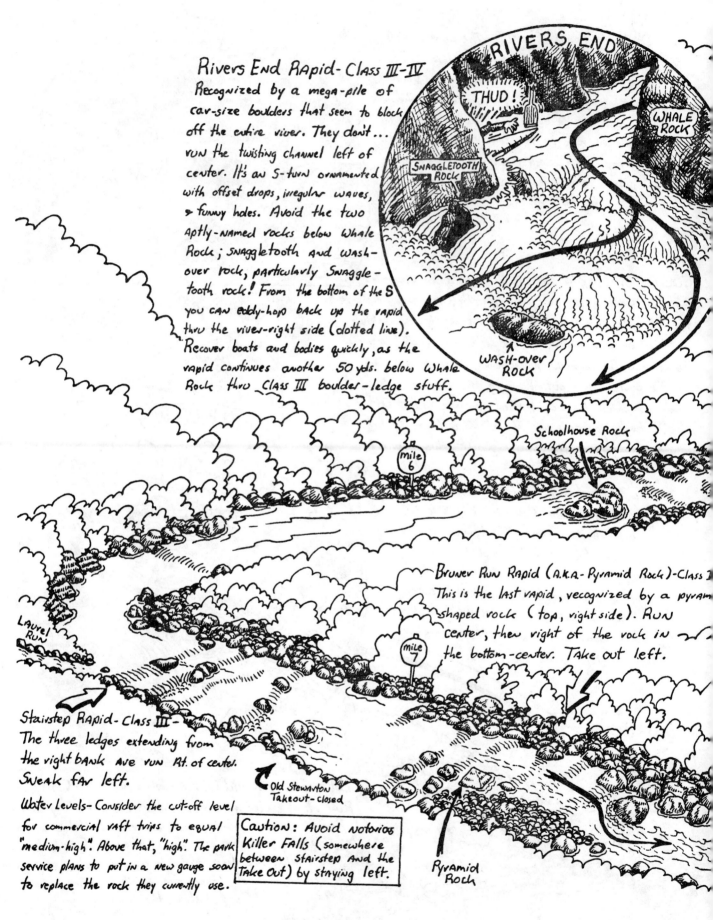

Rivers End Rapid - Class III-IV
Recognized by a mega-pile of
car-size boulders that seem to block
off the entire river. They don't...
run the twisting channel left of
center. It's an S-turn ornamented
with offset drops, irregular waves,
& funny holes. Avoid the two
aptly-named rocks below Whale
Rock; snaggletooth and wash-
over rock, particularly Snaggletooth rock! From the bottom of the S
you can eddy-hop back up the rapid
thru the river-right side (dotted line).
Recover boats and bodies quickly, as the
rapid continues another 50 yds. below Whale
Rock thru Class III boulder-ledge stuff.

RIVERS END

THUD!

WHALE ROCK

SNAGGLETOOTH ROCK

WASH-OVER ROCK

Schoolhouse Rock

mile 6

Laurel Run

Stairstep Rapid - Class III -
The three ledges extending from
the right bank are run Rt. of center.
Sneak far left.

Water Levels - Consider the cut-off level
for commercial raft trips to equal
"medium-high". Above that, "high". The park
service plans to put in a new gauge soon
to replace the rock they currently use.

Old Stewarton
Takeout-closed

mile 7

Bruner Run Rapid (A.K.A.-Pyramid Rock)-Class
This is the last rapid, recognized by a pyram
shaped rock (top, right side). Run
center, then right of the rock in
the bottom-center. Take out left.

Caution: Avoid notorious
Killer Falls (somewhere
between stairstep and the
Take Out) by staying left.

Pyramid Rock

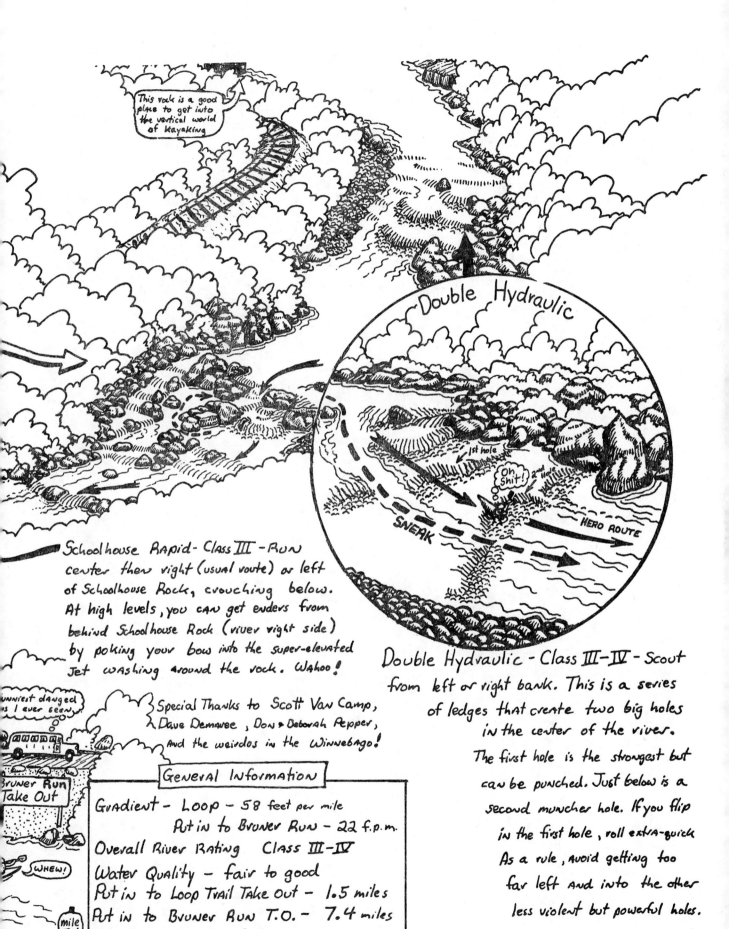

Schoolhouse Rapid - Class III - Run center then right (usual route) or left of Schoolhouse Rock, crouching below. At high levels, you can get enders from behind Schoolhouse Rock (river right side) by poking your bow into the super-elevated Jet washing around the rock. Wahoo!

Special Thanks to Scott Van Camp, Dave Demaree, Don & Deborah Pepper, And the weirdos in the Winnebago!

Double Hydraulic - Class III-IV - Scout from left or right bank. This is a series of ledges that create two big holes in the center of the river.

The first hole is the strongest but can be punched. Just below is a second muncher hole. If you flip in the first hole, roll extra-quick. As a rule, avoid getting too far left and into the other less violent but powerful holes.

General Information

Gradient - Loop - 58 feet per mile
            Put in to Bruner Run - 22 f.p.m.
Overall River Rating Class III-IV
Water Quality - fair to good
Put in to Loop Trail Take Out - 1.5 miles
Put in to Bruner Run T.O. - 7.4 miles
Scenery - excellent!

164